♌   THE LEO ENIGMA   ♌

Cracking the Code

ALSO BY JANE RIDDER-PATRICK

A Handbook of Medical Astrology
Shaping Your Future (Series of 12 titles)
Shaping Your Relationships (Series of 12 titles)

The Zodiac Code series

THE
LEO
ENIGMA

Cracking the Code

23 July – 22 August

Jane Ridder-Patrick

MAINSTREAM
PUBLISHING

EDINBURGH AND LONDON

For my first love

Reprinted 2009

First published in Great Britain in 2004 by
MAINSTREAM PUBLISHING COMPANY
(EDINBURGH) LTD
7 Albany Street
Edinburgh EH1 3UG

ISBN 9781840185294

A catalogue record for this book is available
from the British Library

Typeset in Allise and Van Dijck

Printed in Great Britain by
CPI Antony Rowe, Chippenham, SN14 6LH

Contents

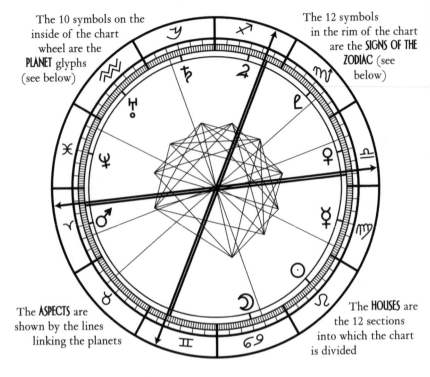

The 10 symbols on the inside of the chart wheel are the **PLANET** glyphs (see below)

The 12 symbols in the rim of the chart are the **SIGNS OF THE ZODIAC** (see below)

The **ASPECTS** are shown by the lines linking the planets

The **HOUSES** are the 12 sections into which the chart is divided

A Sample Birth Chart

Sign	Ruler	Sign	Ruler
Aries ♈	Mars ♂	Libra ♎	Venus ♀
Taurus ♉	Venus ♀	Scorpio ♏	Pluto ♇
Gemini ♊	Mercury ☿	Sagittarius ♐	Jupiter ♃
Cancer ♋	Moon ☽	Capricorn ♑	Saturn ♄
Leo ♌	Sun ☉	Aquarius ♒	Uranus ♅
Virgo ♍	Mercury ☿	Pisces ♓	Neptune ♆

ONE

The Truth of Astrology

MOST PEOPLE'S FIRST EXPERIENCE OF ASTROLOGY IS THROUGH newspapers and magazines. This is a mixed blessing for astrology's reputation – writing an astrology column to any degree of accuracy is a tough, many would say impossible, challenge. The astrologer has to try to say something meaningful about conditions that affect every single person belonging to the same sign, over a very short period of time, in a scant handful of words. The miracle is that some talented astrologers do manage to get across a tantalising whiff of the real thing and keep readers coming back for more of what most of us are hungry for – self-knowledge and reassurance about the future. The downside of the popularity of these columns is that many people think that all astrology is a branch of the entertainment industry and is limited to light-hearted fortune-telling. This is far from the truth.

What Astrology Can Offer

Serious astrology is one of the most sophisticated tools available to help us understand ourselves and the world around us. It gives us a language and a framework to examine and describe – quite literally – *anything* under the Sun, from countries to companies, from money markets to medical matters. Its most common application, however, is in helping people to understand themselves better using their own unique birth charts. Astrology has two main functions. One is to describe the traits and tendencies of whatever it is that is being examined, whether this is a state, a software company or someone's psyche. The other is to give an astonishingly accurate timetable for important changes within that entity. In the chapters that follow, we'll be using astrology to investigate the psychology of the innermost part of your personality, taking a look at what drives, inspires and motivates you.

Astrology uses an ancient system of symbols to describe profound truths about the nature of life on earth, truths that cannot be weighed and measured, but ones we recognise nevertheless, and that touch and move us at a deep level. By linking mythology and mathematics, astrology bridges the gap between our inner lives and our outer experiences, between mind and matter, between poetry and science.

Fate and Free Will

Some people think that astrology is all about foretelling the future, the implication being that everything is predestined and that we have no say in how our lives take shape. None of that is true. We are far from being helpless victims of fate. Everything that happens to us at any given time is the result of past choices. These choices may have been our own, or made by other people. They could even have been made long ago before we, or even our grandparents, were born. It is not always possible to prevent processes that

8

were set in motion in the past from coming to their logical conclusions as events that we then have to deal with. We are, however, all free to decide how to react to whatever is presented to us at every moment of our lives.

Your destiny is linked directly with your personality because the choices you make, consciously or unconsciously, depend largely on your own natural inclinations. It is these inclinations that psychological astrology describes. You can live out every single part of your chart in a constructive or a less constructive way. For instance, if you have Aries strong in your chart, action and initiative will play a major role in your life. It is your choice whether you express yourself aggressively or assertively, heroically or selfishly, and also whether you are the doer or the done-to. Making the right choices is important because every decision has consequences – and what you give out, sooner or later, you get back. If you don't know and understand yourself, you are 'fated' to act according to instinct and how your life experiences have conditioned you. By revealing how you are wired up temperamentally, astrology can highlight alternatives to blind knee-jerk reactions, which often make existing problems worse. This self-knowledge can allow you to make more informed free-will choices, and so help you create a better and more successful future for yourself.

Astrology and Prediction

Astrology cannot predict specific events based on your birth chart. That kind of prediction belongs to clairvoyance and divination. These specialities, when practised by gifted and responsible individuals, can give penetrating insights into events that are likely to happen in the future if matters proceed along their present course.

The real benefit of seeing into the future is that if we don't like what could happen if we carry on the way we're going, we can take steps either to prevent it or to lessen its impact. Rarely is the future chiselled out in stone. There are many possible futures. What you feed with your attention grows. Using your birth chart, a competent astrologer can map out, for years in advance, major turning points, showing which areas of your life will be affected at these times and the kind of change that will be taking place. This information gives answers to the questions that most clients ask in one way or another: 'Why me, why this and why now?' If you accept responsibility for facing what needs to be done at the appropriate time, and doing it, you can change the course of your life for the better.

Astrology and the Soul

What is sometimes called the soul and its purpose is a mystery much more profound than astrology. Most of us have experienced 'chance' meetings and apparent 'tragedies' which have affected the direction of our entire lives. There is an intelligence at work that is infinitely wiser and more powerful than the will or wishes of our small egocentric personalities. This force, whatever name we give it – Universal Wisdom, the Inner Guide, the Self, a guardian angel – steers us into exactly the right conditions for our souls' growth. Astrology can pinpoint the turning points in the course of your destiny and describe the equipment that you have at your disposal for serving, or resisting, the soul's purpose. That equipment is your personality.

Who Are You?

You are no doubt aware of your many good qualities as well as your rather more resistible ones that you might prefer to keep firmly under wraps. Maybe you have wondered why it is that one part of your personality seems to want to do one thing while another part is stubbornly intent on doing the exact opposite. Have you ever wished that you could crack the code that holds the secrets of what makes you – and significant others – behave in the complex way you do? The good news is that you can, with the help of your astrological birth chart, sometimes known as your horoscope.

Just as surely as your DNA identifies you and distinguishes you from everyone else, as well as encoding your peculiarities and potential, your birth chart reveals the unique 'DNA fingerprinting' of your personality. This may seem a staggering claim, but it is one that those who have experienced serious astrology will endorse, so let's take a closer look at what a birth chart is.

Your Birth Chart

Your birth chart is a simplified diagram of the positions of the planets, as seen from the place of your birth, at the moment you took your first independent breath. Critics have said that astrology is obviously nonsense because birth charts are drawn up as if the Sun and all the planets moved round the Earth.

We know in our minds that the Earth moves round the Sun, but that doesn't stop us seeing the Sun rise in the east in the morning and move across the sky to set in the west in the evening. This is an optical illusion. In the same way, we know (or at least most of us know) that we are not really the centre of the universe, but that doesn't stop us experiencing ourselves as being at the focal point of our own personal worlds. It is impossible to live life in any other way. It is the strength, not weakness, of astrology that it describes from your own unique viewpoint how you, as an individual, experience life.

Erecting Your Chart

To draw up a full birth chart you need three pieces of information – the date, time and place of your birth. With your birth date alone you can find the positions of all the planets (except sometimes the Moon) to a good enough degree of accuracy to reveal a great deal of important information about you. If you have the time and place of birth, too, an astrologer can calculate your Ascendant or Rising Sign and the houses of your chart – see below. The Ascendant is a bit like the front door of your personality and describes your general outlook on life. (If you know your Ascendant sign, you might like to read more about its characteristics in the book on that sign in this series.)

The diagram on page 6 shows what a birth chart looks like. Most people find it pretty daunting at first sight but it actually breaks down into only four basic units – the planets, the signs, the aspects and the houses.

The Planets

Below is a simple list of what the planets represent.

PLANET	REPRESENTS YOUR URGE TO
☉ The Sun	express your identity
☽ The Moon	feel nurtured and safe
☿ Mercury	make connections
♀ Venus	attract what you love
♂ Mars	assert your will
♃ Jupiter	find meaning in life
♄ Saturn	achieve your ambitions
♅ Uranus	challenge tradition
♆ Neptune	serve an ideal
♇ Pluto	eliminate, transform and survive

The planets represent the main psychological drives that every single one of us has. The exact way in which we express these drives is not fixed from birth but develops and evolves throughout our lives, both consciously and unconsciously. In this book we will be examining in detail four of these planets – your Sun, Moon, Mercury and Venus. These are the bodies that are right at the heart of our solar system. They correspond, in psychological astrology, to the core of your personality and represent how you express yourself, what motivates you emotionally, how you use your mind and what brings you pleasure.

The Signs
The signs your planets are in show how you tend to express your inner drives. For example, if your Mars is in the action sign of Aries, you will assert yourself pretty directly, pulling no punches. If your Venus is in secretive Scorpio, you will attract, and also be attracted to, emotionally intense relationships. There is a summary of all of the signs on p. 128.

The Aspects
Aspects are important relationships between planets and whether your inner characteristics clash with or complement each other depends largely on whether or not they are in aspect and whether that aspect is an easy or a challenging one. In Chapter Six we'll be looking at some challenging aspects to the Sun.

The Houses
Your birth chart is divided into 12 slices, called houses, each of which is associated with a particular area of life, such as friendships, travel or home life. If, for example, you have your Uranus in the house of career, you are almost

certainly a bit of a maverick at work. If you have your Neptune in the house of partnership, you are likely to idealise your husband, wife or business partner.

The Nature of Time

Your birth chart records a moment in time and space, like a still from a movie – the movie being the apparent movement of the planets round the earth. We all know that time is something that can be measured in precise units, which are always the same, like seconds, months and centuries. But if you stop to reflect for a moment, you'll also recognise that time doesn't always feel the same. Twenty minutes waiting for a bus on a cold, rainy day can seem like a miserable eternity, while the same amount of time spent with someone you love can pass in a flash. As Einstein would say – that's relativity.

There are times in history when something significant seems to be in the air, but even when nothing momentous is happening the quality of time shifts into different 'moods' from moment to moment. Your birth chart is impregnated with the qualities of the time when you were born. For example, people who were born in the mid-to-late 1960s, when society was undergoing major disruptive changes, carry those powerful energies within them and their personalities reflect, in many ways, the turmoil of those troubled and exciting times. Now, as adults, the choices that those individuals make, based on their own inner conflicts and compulsions, will help shape the future of society for better or worse. And so it goes on through the generations.

Seed Meets Soil

There is no such thing as a good or bad chart, nor is any one sign better or worse than another. There are simply 12 different, but equally important, life focuses. It's useful to keep in mind the fact that the chart of each one of us is made up of all the signs of the zodiac. This means that we'll act out, or experience, *every* sign somewhere in our lives. It is true, however, that some individual charts are more challenging than others; but the greater the challenge, the greater the potential for achievement and self-understanding.

In gardening terms, your chart is a bit like the picture on a seed packet. It shows what you could become. If the seeds are of poppies, there's no way you'll get petunias, but external conditions will affect how they grow. With healthy soil, a friendly climate and green-fingered gardeners, the plants have an excellent chance of flourishing. With poor soil, a harsh climate or constant neglect, the seeds will be forced to struggle. This is not always a disadvantage. They can become hardy and adapt, finding new and creative ways of evolving and thriving under more extreme conditions than the plant that was well cared for. It's the same with your chart. The environment you were raised in may have been friendly or hostile to your nature and it will have done much to shape your life until now. Using the insights of astrology to affirm who you are, you can, as an adult, provide your own ideal conditions, become your own best gardener and live out more fully – and successfully – your own highest potential.

TWO

The Symbolism of Leo

ᗡ WE CAN LEARN A GREAT DEAL ABOUT LEO BY LOOKING AT the symbols, myths and legends associated with it. These are time-honoured ways of describing psychological truths; they carry more information than plain facts alone and hint at the deeper meanings and significance of the sign.

The Leo glyph, drawn with a single sweeping stroke, is most commonly seen as the mane, or sometimes the swishing tail, of a lion, Leo's own animal. It also represents an upturned jug, pouring out its contents, just as you, unreservedly, pour out your whole self into projects you believe in. The heart is the organ most closely linked with Leo. The first semi-circle of the glyph is sometimes interpreted as the major vein leading into the heart, the large hoop is the heart itself, and the final up-curve is the great artery which carries the fresh, oxygen-rich blood out into the main circulation to revitalise the body. The passions of your heart are strong, and can include intense pride and desire, as well as the highest and noblest of loves. The first curl can also be seen as a receptacle for divine inspiration, while the main loop is the personality, which receives and contains it, and the final upstroke is the outflow of that same power, now radiating through the individual. This refers to Leo's highest role as dispenser of love and authority. In earlier times, kings and queens, who are closely associated with the royal sign of Leo, were seen as representatives of God on earth.

Leo the Lion

The Lion may be linked with Leo because in ancient Egypt, where much of western astrology has its roots, the River Nile rose and flooded the surrounding countryside when the Sun entered the constellation of Leo. This brought fertility and abundance as it allowed crops to grow and, at that time, the lions left their desert homes and came to refresh themselves beside the cool waters. In Rome, the lion was the symbol of imperial might. The lion represents dignity, strength and majesty, as well as spiritual power and wisdom. The lion, however, also has a darker side, and in the Bible the devil is compared to a roaring lion 'seeking whom he may devour'. The apt expression for a group of lions is a pride of lions – pride often being Leo's downfall – but it is also the quality that can prevent you acting unworthily. Whether you live out the nobler or baser type of Leo behaviour depends on what is more important to you – enhancing your own ego or serving something higher.

Each of the four fixed signs – Taurus, Leo, Scorpio and Aquarius – is linked with a Christian evangelist. These are St Luke, St Mark, St John and St Matthew, respectively. St Mark, who stressed Christ's power and royalty, is often shown as a winged lion.

Leo in Myth and Legend

The first labour of the hero, Hercules, was to kill and skin the Nemean Lion that was destroying every living creature in the surrounding area. It was an enormous beast whose pelt was resistant to iron, bronze and stone. Hercules tried to kill it with a sword, a club and then arrows. None of these had any effect. To kill it, he had to trap it in its own cave and wrestle it to death with his bare hands. He then removed its skin, which he wore to make him invulnerable during his subsequent arduous tasks.

This story shows the major challenge of Leo's life. Your turning point comes when you wrestle with your ego, powerful passions and instinct to dominate – represented by the wild, destructive lion. Then you can invest that powerful energy in the service of others, in the same way that the hero puts on the lion's skin to help him carry out his Herculean work, that so benefited the world.

The Constellation of Leo

The constellation of Leo is one of the brightest in the sky. Like you, it is hard to overlook. At the heart of the lion is the royal star, Regulus, which means little king. Regulus is actually made up of three stars, but appears to the naked eye as one. People whose charts have Regulus prominent are, according to traditional astrology, likely to reach high positions and associate with rulers or famous people.

Leo's Ruling Planet

Each sign is associated with a planet, which is called its ruler. Leo is ruled by the Sun, the star at the centre of our solar system. It radiates energy in the form of heat and light, and all of the other planets revolve around it. That's reflected in the way you live your life, sharing your warmth and brightness freely and enjoying being at the centre of attention. Apollo, the ancient Greek god of the Sun, was patron of the arts and sciences and was worshipped at Delphi. People used to come from far and wide to enquire of the prophetess, who sat in his shrine, for insight into their problems, rather like the way people today often look to Leos for guidance and leadership.

Another mythical figure associated with the Sun was Helios, who drove his chariot across the skies from his magnificent palace in the far east at dawn to his equally magnificent palace in the far west at sunset. (He took an underworld ferry back east overnight.) One day he gave in to the nagging of his son, Phaethon, who wanted to drive the chariot. Phaeton really just wanted to show off, and didn't have the expertise to control the horses. He first of all drove so high into the sky that the earth went cold, then he came so near that the fields were scorched. Zeus, the chief god, lost his temper and killed him with a thunderbolt. The moral of this story for Leos is this: exhibitionism and pretending to be better than you are can bring you down to earth with a bang.

The Season of Leo

In the northern hemisphere, Leo's season is midsummer, when the rays of the Sun are at their most intense. It's often too hot to work so, for country folk, it can be the time to take a break and enjoy themselves, while gathering strength for the harvest to come. For children, school is out and it's the holiday season, a chance for most people to relax and have fun, away from the duties of everyday life. With your sunny Leo nature, it's summertime all the year round . . .

THREE

The Heart of the Sun

O THE GLYPH FOR THE SUN IS A PERFECT CIRCLE WITH A DOT in the centre and symbolises our dual nature – earthly and eternal. The circle stands for the boundary of the personality, which distinguishes and separates each individual from every other individual, for it is our differences from other people that make us unique, not our similarities. The dot in the centre indicates the mysterious 'divine spark' within us and the potential for becoming conscious of who we truly are, where we have come from and what we may become.

The Meaning of the Sun

Each of your planets represents a different strand of your personality. The Sun is reckoned to be the most important factor of your whole birth chart. It describes your sense of identity, and the sign that the Sun was in when you were born, your Sun sign, along with its house position and any aspects to other planets, shows how you express and develop that identity.

Your Role in Life

Each of the signs is associated with certain roles that can be played in an infinite number of ways. Take one of the roles of Aries, which is the warrior. A warrior can cover anything from Attila the Hun, who devastated vast stretches of Europe with his deliberate violence, to an eco-warrior, battling to save the environment. The role, warrior, is the same; the motivation and actions are totally different. You can live out every part of your personality in four main ways – as creator, destroyer, onlooker or victim. How you act depends on who you choose to be from the endless variations possible from the symbolism of each of your planets, but most particularly your Sun. And you do have a choice; not all Geminis are irresponsible space cadets nor is every Scorpio a sex-crazed sadist. This book aims to paint a picture of what some of your choices might be and show what choices, conscious or unconscious, some well-known people of your sign have made.

Your upbringing will have helped shape what you believe about yourself and out of those beliefs comes, automatically, behaviour to match. For example, if you believe you are a victim, you will behave like one and the world will happily oblige by victimising you. If you see yourself as a carer, life will present you with plenty to care for – and often to care about, too. If you identify yourself as an adventurer, you'll spot opportunities at every corner. If you're a winner, then you'll tend to succeed. Shift the way that you see yourself and your whole world shifts, too.

Your Vocation

Your Sun describes your major life focus. This is not always a career. As the poet Milton said: 'They also serve who only stand and wait.' It is impossible to tell from your Sun sign exactly what your calling is – there are people of all signs occupied in practically every area of life. What is important is not so much *what* you do, but the way that you do it and it is this – how you express yourself – that your Sun describes. If you spend most of your time working at an occupation or living in a situation where you can't give expression to the qualities of your Sun, or which forces you to go against the grain of your Sun's natural inclinations, then you're likely to live a life of quiet, or possibly even noisy, desperation.

On Whose Authority

Your personality, which your birth chart maps, is like a sensitive instrument that will resonate only to certain frequencies – those that are similar to its own. Your Sun shows the kind of authority that will strike a chord with you, either positively or negatively, because it is in harmony with yours. It can show how you relate to people in authority, especially your father. (It is the Moon that usually shows the relationship with your mother and home.) In adult life it can throw light onto the types of bosses you are likely to come across, and also how you could react to them. It is a major part of the maturing process to take responsibility for expressing your own authority wisely. When you do so, many of your problems with external authorities diminish or even disappear.

In a woman's chart the Sun can also describe the kind of husband she chooses. This is partly because, traditionally, a husband had legal authority over his wife. It is also because, especially in the early years of a marriage, many women choose to pour their energies into homemaking and supporting their husbands' work in the world rather than their own and so his career becomes her career. As a Leo, you may find that your father, boss or husband shows either the positive or negative traits of Leo or, as is usually the case, a mixture of both – generous, warm-hearted and dramatic or attention-seeking, pompous and dictatorial.

Born on the Cusp

If you were born near the beginning or end of Leo, you may know that your birthday falls on the cusp, or meeting point, of two signs. The Sun, however, can only be in one sign or the other. You can find out for sure which sign your Sun is in by checking the tables on pp. 97–8.

FOUR

The Drama of Being a Leo

EACH SIGN IS ASSOCIATED WITH A CLUSTER OF ROLES THAT HAVE their own core drama or storyline. Being born is a bit like arriving in the middle of an ongoing play and slipping into a certain part. How we play our characters is powerfully shaped in early life by having to respond to the input of the other actors around us – the people that make up our families and communities. As the play of our lives unfolds, we usually become aware that there are themes which tend to repeat themselves. We may ask ourselves questions like 'Why do I always end up with all the work / caught up in fights / with partners who mistreat me / in dead-end jobs / successful but unhappy . . .?' or whatever. Interestingly, I've found that people are less likely to question the wonderful things that happen to them again and again.

The good news is that once we recognise the way we have been playing our roles, we can then use our free-will choice to do some creative re-scripting, using the same character in more constructive scenarios. Even better news is that if we change, the other people in our dramas have got to make some alterations, too. If you refuse to respond

24

to the same old cues in the customary ways, they are going to have to get creative too.

Leos are often given a bad press, being described as self-absorbed exhibitionists with god complexes. While there are undoubtedly some Leos like that around, the underlying astrological truth is much more interesting. Above the shrine of the Sun god, Apollo, were inscribed the words 'Man, Know Thyself'. The complete phrase is 'Man, know thyself and ye shall know God'. This is your business as a Leo – to make the journey to the centre of the self to try to find answers to the question 'Who am I?'

In many mystical traditions it is said that, In the beginning, there was the One, and the One longed to know itself in all its glorious forms, and to be seen and praised by its own creations. As the Scottish poet Robert Burns said, 'O wad some power the giftie gie us, to see ourselves as others see us.' And it so happened that God, or whatever we like to call the source of life, had the power to give itself just that giftie. So God created many different aspects of Him/Her/Itself in the form of humans, animals, plants and minerals. We humans, being made in the likeness of God, were given consciousness to reflect on ourselves, and on our actions. We were also given the capacity to create – which is the ability to express outwardly who we are and what we have within ourselves. Some traditions talk of humans, in the birth process, going through the spheres of each of the planets, and taking on the quality of each in turn. By the time we are born, we have forgotten who we are and experience ourselves as separate units, cut off from everyone else in our individual casings of skin. The purpose of life, then, is to find out who we are and where we have come from. The philosopher Alan Watts calls this God playing hide-and-seek with itself. Interestingly, recent discoveries about the composition of the waters of the womb show that it actually does contain a chemical that induces memory loss.

All of the signs of the zodiac, according to esoteric thought, are aspects of the divine and the aspect, or role, that Leos live out is that of the performer, acting out parts of themselves so that they can get to know and glory in themselves. Just as it is impossible to know what we look like without some kind of mirror, so you, as a Leo, can't know yourself properly without seeing the reflection of yourself in the eyes of other people. You need their feedback to let you know who you are, and how you are doing – hence the powerful urge to create and perform to an audience, preferably an admiring one.

Most Leos are unlikely to have trouble with the notion of being an aspect of God. You may, however, have rather more difficulty acknowledging, or even recognising, that other people are too. Some immature Leos aren't always clear about the distinction between being a representative of the divine in human form, with all the imperfections that that implies, and *being* God. Once you move beyond this stage and serve something higher than your own ego, you are truly stellar. When your mettle has been tested and found to be true gold, in the 'real' world outside of your imagination, and when, through experience and failure, you have learned compassion and consideration for others, then you will have acquired the finest that Leo has to offer – a nobility, combined with generosity, that brings radiance to all that it touches, just as the king's touch was once thought to heal every ill.

Other Leo roles are the ruler, creator, star, director, representative, ambassador, storyteller and dramatist – roles which involve being centre-stage or at the hub of any enterprise, directing the whole show.

How you choose to see your role will determine your behaviour. The following chapter describes some typical Leo behaviour. Remember, though, that there is no such thing as a person who is all Leo and nothing but Leo. You are much more complicated than that and other parts of your chart will modify, or may even seem to contradict, the single, but central, strand of your personality which is your Sun sign. These other sides of your nature will add colour and contrast and may restrict or reinforce your basic Leo identity. They won't, however, cancel out the challenges you face as a Leo.

FIVE

The Leo Temperament

THERE IS NOTHING PETTY OR MEAN-SPIRITED ABOUT YOU. YOU always think big. No one can match you in generosity, whether it's money, time or personal presence. You love to dispense bounty and usually much prefer to give lavishly than to receive, though you do resent expectations or demands on you, or – perish the thought – having your contribution taken for granted. Frequently you're the first to put your hand in your pocket when the bill is presented in company. But it's good to remember that receiving, with graciousness and appreciation, can also be a form of generosity, allowing others the chance to feel the joy and pride of giving, no matter how small the gift.

You rarely hold back with advice either. Often this is astute and much appreciated, but you can be hurt to the quick if your unsolicited help is ignored or rejected, as you genuinely mean well. It may take a hard knock or two to show that there is a definite line between sensitive and appropriate assistance and plain interfering because you believe you know better than the recipient what's in their own best interests. It upsets you if help or advice that you

28

have given later proves to be wrong or disappointing, as you feel that this is a direct and unflattering reflection on you.

It's Only Money

Open-handed and at times wildly extravagant, you can be splashy and a bit of a gambler unless there are more cautious and restrained factors in your chart. Like a child, you live in the present tense and aren't prone to linger too long on what's over and done with. As for the future – you're quite content to let that take care of itself. You've the happy knack of seizing the moment and extracting from it every last drop of pleasure. You love the finest of everything and want it all – power, prestige, money and love – and there is no reason at all why you shouldn't have it either. In some Leos, however, this conviction of being entitled to first-class and luxury can lead to an inflated sense of their own importance – together with the attitude that other people are inferior beings, a view which is prone to bring out the killer instincts of everyone within put-down range. Limits are irritants, if you notice them at all, and until you've learned that little gnomes don't come and replenish your coffers overnight, you may not even bother to check if there is anything in the bank to cover expenses.

I Know Where I'm Going

Indecision rarely troubles you, as you are so spontaneous. You know what you want out of life and you set out with energy and sheer, unabashed determination to commandeer it. You've an uncanny knack of getting what you want, probably because it never occurs to you that you won't get it. Madonna commented that a lot of people are afraid to say what they want – which is why they don't get what they want. Those people she was referring to, of course, are unlikely to be Leos. She was speaking for her sign when she remarked, 'When I'm hungry, I eat. When I'm thirsty, I drink. When I feel like saying something, I say it.' Just like a child – or a Zen master.

Straight from the Heart

The source of all your self-confidence is that you are tuned into the dictates of your heart, so you don't have to look to any authority from the outside. What is heartfelt is true and, unless you have some darker components in your chart, you are utterly sincere in all that you do. With a touching faith in yourself, and in essential human goodness, your intention is usually to act honourably. So you can be an easy target for the unscrupulous, who may take advantage of your openness, which can verge on naivety. If you are let down, you can feel completely at a loss because calculated meanness is rarely in your repertoire and often you simply don't understand it. You might possibly indulge in a moment's cynicism, but this will seldom congeal into bitterness. Soon the sun will come out from behind the clouds, and all will be well again. With your spontaneously combustible joy, you can put heart into others, just as the light and warmth of the sun magics away darkness and cold. On good days, which are most days, life is a celebration, as you love pleasure and can be rather self-indulgent. When you entertain, you do so in style, creating a fitting backdrop for your sparkling personality.

The Cowardly Lion

Underneath that confident front, Leo is actually one of the most vulnerable signs. You can secretly worry that, when it comes to the crunch, you'll lack courage, lose heart and fail. Worse, you'll be found out as being only ordinary and not at all special – your secret worst nightmare. Just as a match doesn't light until it strikes against something hard and rough, you only find out what you're made of when you're under duress. Crises bring out the best in you and it's a rare Leo who doesn't rise to the occasion. You have the strength and will to meet with courage, intelligence and dignity all that life presents you with. Like a flame reaching upward, you aspire to be bigger and greater than who you are now and, by doing so, you can actually become what you aim to be. The phrase 'fake it till you make it' could have been coined specially for you.

The Royal We

You are a natural aristocrat and respond to everything that is honourable and magnificent. Each sign can learn from the one opposite, which in your case is Aquarius. Add a measure of democracy to your fiery individuality and you have the makings of greatness. A monarch's true role is to serve his or her people. Queen Elixabeth II, who has her Moon in Leo, has lived this out to a remarkable degree. You are born to rule and command but to do that well there are conditions. The French have a phrase for this – *noblesse oblige* – meaning that with nobility come obligations. Real success comes when your personal ambitions are linked with the common good.

It's all too easy for you not to notice how much work and inconvenience you are creating for others by being so focused on your own affairs. Princess Margaret used to smoke all through dinner, party late into the night, expecting no one to leave before her, oblivious to the fact that others had jobs to go to in the morning and that the staff could not go to bed until she was safely home. Yet, despite such inconsiderate behaviour, her closest friends remained fiercely loyal right to the end because of the warmth, fun and generosity of her personality.

Like royalty, you know your place – and you expect others to remember theirs too. You don't care to be treated with familiarity by strangers or underlings. If others overstep your mark, they can expect a chilly response. You can be a tad snobbish and may even ignore, or overlook, people that you feel are beneath your station. You prefer to mingle with those who are distinguished in some way, either by merit or rank, basking in the glory that rubs off on you. Some Leos are so concerned with the outer shows of greatness – like money, power and glamour – that they don't bother to look beneath the surface to see if a person or situation has any genuine worth. They forget that all that glitters isn't gold and that authentic aristocracy is aristocracy of the spirit. As the Leo poet Alfred, Lord Tennyson, wrote: 'Kind hearts are more than coronets'.

Eternal Flames

You are like a steadily glowing fire, warm and dramatic, giving your light and heat to all that come near. It depends on what feeds your flame whether your boundless vitality is used for good or ill. Some insecure Leos can go astray and, instead of radiating sunshine and encouraging others, they are like black holes sucking all glory and authority towards themselves. They become conceited tyrants and attention-seekers, like Mussolini or Napoleon, domineering and destroying everything that stands in the way of their becoming masters and mistresses of the universe. Think of the once-noble kings in *The Lord of the Rings*, who gave in to the temptation of possessing the ring of power. They lost their souls to the dark lord in their lust for personal gain. When in doubt about any action, the question to ask

is: 'What does this serve – my own ego, or truth and love?'
The good news is that, no matter how deep the darkness
into which they have fallen, when Leos decide to move
towards the light, which is where the lion belongs, they
make lightning-quick progress.

As Within, So Without

You are intensely self-conscious, constantly in front of some
mirror or other. Even if you are a shy or introverted Leo
(yes, they do exist), you are acutely aware of the impact
you are making on others. Your entries and exits are well
stage-managed. In your attempts to show yourself in the
most favourable light, you'll study what you can do to make
the most powerful dramatic effect, and adjust your
behaviour accordingly. Because solitary reflection and self-
analysis is hard for you, you are heavily dependent on the
response of others to know how you are doing. Needing
this input so much, you're inclined to draw attention to
yourself. Depending on your degree of subtlety, your
methods can be anything from maintaining a beautifully
turned-out appearance and gracious manners, to eye-
poppingly ostentatious dress and behaviour, right through
to crowbarring evidence of your own importance and
achievements into every conversation you have.

Approving of Yourself

Your performances are, at core, not really about creating a
show for others to applaud, but attempts to answer the
question 'Who am I?'. You have an urge to express yourself
– to push little bits of what is in you out into the world,
and watch how the world responds to them. Self-knowledge
comes by seeing yourself through the eyes of others.
Although you have a craving to be admired and well

thought-of, the most important approval is self-approval and, unless you are very insecure, if you think a certain course of action is right, you will take it and public opinion can go hang. When doing and saying what is true, loving and from the heart is more important to you than other people's good opinion, you've truly found your bliss. As Leo writer Paul Tillich wrote: 'Joy is the emotional expression of the courageous Yes to one's own true being.' And you have that courage in abundance.

Self-Service

Your favourite subject, and most important relationship, is with yourself. Because you experience yourself as central and consider everything in terms of your own interests, it is difficult – and painful – to accept that others are different and think differently from you and that they have a right to be and do so. You tend to treat others as an extension of yourself and if people don't side with you in just about everything, you can look on this as downright disloyalty. Hard as it is for you to adjust to the reality of others, if you don't make an attempt to see their point of view you may find that they withdraw, leaving you hurt and bewildered as to why that happened. Peter O'Toole thought he was happily married until his wife left him – evidently her perspective on the matter differed markedly from his.

Flattery and Frankness

Because it's hard for you to put yourself in another's shoes, you can sometimes be, unwittingly, rather too frank and tactless. You don't like criticism much yourself so, to be heard, any adverse comments heading your way must be dished up with double portions of butter and honey. As you take everything so much to heart, and feel deeply, you are heartbroken if you're not appreciated and, if your dignity is ruffled, you can either put others down with cold contempt or, alternatively, explode with rage. You can take yourself far too seriously, so developing a sense of humour and learning to laugh at yourself is an excellent investment to help you lighten up.

Flattery could get people almost anywhere with you. Since you want to believe nice things about yourself, you can be fooled by insincere compliments and even out-and-out lies which feed your need for praise and honour. With your burning need to express *all* of yourself, unless other parts of your chart indicate secrecy – a Scorpio Moon for instance – you tend to be completely open about yourself and your affairs, and can't understand those who aren't. As you enjoy a good gossip too, you hate to be left out of anything, especially insider information. Your creativity and sense of drama can make you an excellent storyteller and, to enhance the effect, you may be tempted to add a few choice embellishments that may lack strict factual accuracy but almost invariably bathe you in a subtle, but unmistakable, halo effect.

Leo at Work

Playing second fiddle or working quietly behind the scenes is not your style. Being in charge of your own affairs and working on ideas and projects at your own pace is what you do best, preferably assisted by a band of loyal and willing helpers – like a star surrounded by satellites. You like to put the stamp of your individuality on all of your work. That includes the input of others under your authority, who must be prepared to be seen as your product. Alfred Hitchcock's signature was a tiny cameo performance in each of his own films.

You'll Do It My Way

With unflinching faith in the success of whatever you touch, you lead and inspire by example and charisma, influencing others by the sheer force of your personality. Often what you are promoting is less important than the way you do it, with your dramatic style and arm-around-the-shoulder magnanimous gestures. A natural leader, in an emergency you are unsurpassed. You love organising and are first-class at delegating, especially those unseen but essential jobs that are messy, boring, repetitive and unglamorous. An ordered life is what you're after, provided, of course, that you are the one issuing the orders. Being ambitious, with a flair for self-promotion, you can be a bit of a benign dictator, taking the line that it's 'my way or the highway'. If you are allowed to get away with it, you can easily slide towards laziness and despotism. Thinking that everything should automatically come your way, you'll then let everyone else fetch and carry while you, unashamedly, take the lion's share of the recognition – and the profits.

Creative Copyright

You may have the infuriating Leo habit of annexing and taking credit for other people's ideas and creativity, then trying to make them feel petty when they object. This is no way to win friends and influence people. Alexandre Dumas, author of *The Three Musketeers*, was a notable example of a blatant literary thief. He filched ideas from everywhere quite brazenly and then stamped his own giant personality on the work of others. But, as the saying goes, to copy one person's work is plagiarism, but to steal from many – well, that's research.

Born to be Great

Titles, status and prestige appeal to you, the bigger and glossier the better. If you are not promoted quickly, you'll move on but, as long as you have power, authority and respect – and preferably framed awards to prove it – you will work your heart out to live up to your position and the trust others put in you. If you are overlooked or discouraged at work, you'll lose interest and hang around lazily, filing your nails and yawning, which is a criminal waste of your talent. As you like feedback, any job where you are performing and making an instant impact is right up your street. The stage is an obvious choice, as is art – painting, drama, storytelling and teaching. Young Leos are natural showmen and women and make excellent promoters. Because you can spot the potential in almost any situation, and you trust your hunches, you can make an excellent entrepreneur. When your energy and resources are focused and well-directed, your achievements can be colossal and your work can influence large numbers of people, usually for the good. C.G. Jung, the twentieth-century giant of depth psychology, Henry Ford, father of production-line cars, John Logie Baird, inventor of television and Cecil B. de Mille, with his spectacular cast-of-thousands movies, were all Leo greats.

Leo and Health

You are a powerhouse of energy and your stamina can be phenomenal, but if you feel unappreciated your physical health could suffer, especially in the three main areas associated with Leo – the heart, back and eyes. Symbolically, the spine and back represent integrity and standing up for, and living by, what you know is right. The heart represents the ability to give and receive love, and the eyes symbolise vision – both the ability to see what is staring you right in the face and the potential for visualising the future. Psychological imbalances in these areas can lead to Leo ailments, or problems with the bowels, circulation or thyroid gland. Attending to these matters can often result in a speedy recovery.

Leo Relating

It's a rare Leo who is not in, or just out of, love. For you, love is not just a many-splendoured thing; it is truly what makes your world go round. When you love, you do so wholeheartedly and you can consume your loved ones with the unrelenting flames of your burning passion. If you love someone, you will move heaven and earth for him or her. Where love is lacking, you may simply use others for your own gratification, as ego or elbow decorations.

Making a Splash

You like your romances big, dramatic and theatrical, and the spectacular gifts you lavish on your love can sometimes be as much to impress onlookers with your taste and style as to woo your partner. You're wonderful with the props of passion – flowers, scents, champagne and candlelit dinners. Being idealistic, you believe in magic; a beautiful love affair followed by the sumptuous wedding in a fairy-tale castle (either real or in the air) and then walking into the sunset to live happily ever after in unruffled marital bliss. Life, therefore, sometimes has a few surprises waiting for you . . .

Doing You Proud

You want a partner that you can be proud of, one who makes you feel good and who will show you in a good light by association – preferably someone glamorous, vivacious and good-looking, with bags of charm, warmth and sex appeal. Power, personality and position help too. It's important that you feel your mate is worthy to share, and enhance, your sense of self. If you fall into the Leo trap of failing to see your lover as a person separate from you, but rather as an audience or player in your drama, your mate could then feel left out of the partnership equation. You like to be the most important one in the relationship and may feel threatened by a partner shining brighter than you. Insecure Leos whose partners become more successful or get more recognition than them can turn very sour indeed and may resort to subtly cruel, undermining behaviour to elbow themselves back into the limelight. Confident Leos, however, not only acknowledge a partner's need for independence and a life that doesn't merely revolve around them; they are actively encouraging, and supportive to the hilt.

Earthing Your Fire

Leos are often attracted to people who have the earth signs strong in their charts, as they are gifted at dealing with the practical matters that often you are not. Once committed, you are devoted and you expect love to be returned with equal ardour and loyalty. Security and peace are important to you and, like lions in ancient times, which were kept as pets in aristocratic households, you can settle very happily into being cosseted and domesticated. You make a strong, supportive and protective, if rather bossy, partner but can be demanding and sometimes a little selfish, expecting attention, freedom and unlimited ego-stroking.

Sexual Satisfaction

In sex, appearance and drama often matter more to you than physical attraction alone. With your vivid imagination, erotic images can turn you on wildly, but the everyday realities and imperfections of the flesh, like cellulite, flatulence and fumbling for contraceptives, can be major turn-offs. Unless you have matured and come to terms with life on planet earth, once the romance stage has passed – which is the part you enjoy – you could start to take the relationship for granted. Worse, if they become bored, some thoughtless Leos have been known to abandon used lovers like empty banana skins, while blaming the other person for not being perfect. You may operate a double standard, doing exactly what you like but feeling abandoned and betrayed if your partner ever puts his or her own interests before your own. Betrayal is deeply wounding and rarely forgotten. Infidelity, in your eyes, is high treason, though you will overlook it if you know that you are still the centre of your partner's world and the third party is simply a bit of amusement indulged in on the side. Although you are a natural flirt yourself, you can become jealous if your partner looks elsewhere, as you are terrified of the loss of love and attention. By inclination rather lazy, you are more likely to be faithful than not – why go to the bother of hunting if you have enough at home? – unless opportunities are thrust right under your nose. You are also extremely loyal and idealistic and, for you, a promise is a promise . . .

SIX

Aspects of the Sun

PLANETS, JUST LIKE PEOPLE, CAN HAVE IMPORTANT RELATIONSHIPS with each other. These relationships are called aspects. Aspects to your Sun from any other planet can influence your personality markedly. The most powerful effects come with those from the slower-moving planets – Saturn, Uranus, Neptune or Pluto. Sometimes they can alter your ideas about yourself and your behaviour patterns so much that you may not feel at all typical of your sign in certain areas of your life.

Check if your birth date and year appear in the various sections below to find out if one or more of these planets was aspecting the Sun when you were born. Only the so-called challenging aspects have been included. These are formed when the planets are together, opposite or at right angles to each other in the sky.

Unfortunately, because space is restricted, other aspects have been left out, although they have similar effects to those described below and, for the same reason, a few dates will inevitably have been missed out, too. (You can find out for sure whether or not your Sun is aspected at my website

41

www.janeridderpatrick.com) If your Sun has no aspects to Saturn, Uranus, Neptune or Pluto, you're more likely to be a typical Leo.

Some well-known Leos with challenging aspects to their Suns appear below. You can find more in the birthday section at the end of the book.

Sun in Leo in Aspect with Saturn

If you were born between 1946 and 1948, or 1976 and 1978, whether or not your birthday is listed below, you are likely to feel the influence of Saturn on your Sun.

22 July–2 August in: 1932, 1939, 1946, 1954, 1962, 1969, 1976, 1983–4, 1991 and 1998

3–13 August in: 1933, 1940, 1947, 1955, 1963, 1970, 1977, 1984–5, 1992 and 1999

14–23 August in: 1934, 1941, 1948, 1956, 1963–4, 1970, 1977–8, 1985, 1993 and 2000

| John Logie Baird | Whitney Houston | Beatrix Potter |
| Arnold Schwarzenegger | Sir Walter Scott | Jacqueline Susann |

Your powerful ambition to get on in the world, make a name for yourself and to be recognised as an authority in your field can certainly become a reality – provided you avoid a few common pitfalls. If you expect an effortless path to success and riches, paved with gold and strewn with rose petals, think again. Whatever you do, though, don't be disheartened, become cynical or simply give up. Wherever Saturn is around, you have to work your passage and expect a few learning experiences en route. If you accept those conditions with grace, you are well on your way to the top. The more you push yourself onward and upward without considering others – or practical realities – the harder you could fall from time to time. Sir Walter Scott achieved fame and fortune as one of Europe's great literary figures, but he overstretched himself by building a gothic mansion and investing in a publishing business that failed. With true Leo pride, he swore to pay back every one of his creditors. This he did by writing prolifically for years on end.

You've a tendency, that you'll probably hide, to feel inadequate or self-critical. Any time your inner judge tries to put you down, just talk back and ask it for some sensible advice instead; the chances are you will get it. Hard work, discipline and coming to terms with life's limitations pay off with this aspect. Trying to take shortcuts to success will not. You'll only be truly happy when you stop seeking approval from others. Set your own goals and put all your efforts into attaining them. Then you'll find the Leo combination of integrity, leadership and worldly realism can lead to very rich rewards indeed.

Sun in Leo in Aspect with Uranus

If you were born between 1955 and 1962, whether or not your birthday is listed below, you are likely to feel the influence of Uranus on your Sun.

22 July–2 August in: 1934–7, 1955–8 and 1975–7
3–13 August in: 1936–9, 1957–60 and 1978–80
14–23 August in: 1939–41, 1960–62 and 1980–82

Louise Brown	Melanie Griffith	Dustin Hoffman
Mata Hari	Sean Penn	Percy Bysshe Shelley

One thing is sure – you will stand out as being different in some way. Leo enjoys being noticed and Uranus itches to challenge the accepted way of doing things. Not many of you, though, will be as cutting-edge as Louise Brown, who was the world's first test-tube baby. There is part of you that can delight in flouting convention and some of you may be interested in, or even work with, new technologies, humanitarian projects or ideas that are different from the norm or way ahead of their time. Others may see you as an innovator or reformer, or even a bit of an oddball – not that that would worry you.

You can be hugely self-willed – even downright bloody-minded; both Uranus and the Sun in Leo are a touch autocratic and can overlook the opinions and feelings of other people. You may have strong ideas on how things should be and will push forward relentlessly, insisting on going your own way. Often you will be right, as you've the knack of analysing a system and being able to pinpoint where it is flawed or outdated. As you have the confidence to believe in your own vision, you'll either spearhead the cause yourself or encourage others to do so. Settling down conventionally, either to a career or a relationship, may prove challenging. Learning a little tolerance can help you make the best of this exciting combination. Whatever else you are, you are certainly not dull. Women with this aspect need a great deal of freedom and often prefer to have partners who are out from under their feet, and possibly away from home, much of the time so that they can have plenty of breathing space.

Sun in Leo in Aspect with Neptune

22 July–2 August in: 1956–62 and 1998–2000
3–13 August in: 1961–8
14–23 August in: 1966–71

Halle Berry	Fidel Castro	Coco Chanel
Ted Hughes	C.G. Jung	J.K. Rowling

Neptune, planet of self-sacrifice, fantasy and yearning, combined with the regal Sun in Leo can be a potent mix. Others can put you on a pedestal and look up to you as some kind of demi-god, not able to see the real person behind the layers of illusion they have wrapped you in. Part of you may enjoy the experience, but if you start to believe the fantasies about yourself, you are in deep trouble. As the great Swiss psychologist C.G. Jung once said, 'Thank goodness I'm Jung and not a Jungian.'

Some, like Coco Chanel, are purveyors of glamour and you could do well in jobs where glossy images of luxury and perfection are created, like fashion, advertising and the film industry. On the downside, though, you may not always have a clear sense of who you are. To help build up an identity, some with this combination mingle with the great and the good, hoping that a little prestige rubs off on them. You may enjoy losing yourself by pretending to be someone else, either in your daydreams or in real life. It's best not to be drawn into losing yourself in mind-altering substances, as you are highly susceptible to addictions.

You may idealise your father but feel that he is somehow just out of reach. Alternatively, like Jung, you could find him weak and rather a disappointment.

Many with this aspect love the arts and if you aren't a poet or painter yourself, you'll support those who are. You may be drawn to mysticism, spirituality or charitable works, dedicating yourself to developing the highest qualities in yourself and others, or, like J.K. Rowling, helping alleviate suffering by generous donations of your time, energy or money.

Sun in Leo in Aspect with Pluto

If you were born between 1938 and 1957, even if your birthday does not appear in the list below, the following is likely to apply to you to a greater or lesser extent. Pluto was going through Leo in those years, producing what is known as the 'Me Generation'.

22 July–2 August in: 1938–1946 and 1984–8
3–13 August in: 1945–53 and 1988–93
14–23 August in: 1952–9 and 1992–6

Princess Anne	Mick Jagger	David Koresh
Madonna	Helen Mirren	George Bernard Shaw

Pluto means power and you'll either wield it yourself or could feel it used against you at some time in your life. You are a force to be reckoned with and can transform the world around you for good or ill. Some with this aspect cannot tolerate the misuse of rank and power and will speak out and act against it courageously, like Princess Anne who, while on the Olympic Games committee, would not overlook deviations from honourable practice. At the other extreme are those who combine Leo arrogance and plutonic paranoia. Mercifully, this rarely results in the kind of tragedy caused by cult leader David Koresh, whose gospel was 'If the Bible is true, I am Jesus Christ.' His followers had to live strictly chaste and simple lives while he indulged himself, especially sexually, with 19 wives. He barricaded himself in at Waco with his followers, stockpiling weapons, waiting for the end of the world, and in the showdown with the FBI almost 100 people, including him, were killed.

Your life is likely to have several total endings and new beginnings where you rise, like the phoenix, from the ashes of your old existence and completely reinvent yourself.

This periodic transformation is simply part of who you are. Few, however, do it as spectacularly or as publicly as Madonna, who has grown from brattishness to brilliance, earning bravos all round. There is often a touch of ruthlessness and formidable self-belief with this aspect and you may find yourself in relationships involving intense power struggles, some of them provoked or made worse by your attitude, conscious or unconscious, of 'nobody pushes me around'. Peace comes when you stop trying to control the world and learn to trust life.

SEVEN

Meeting Your Moon

D THE GLYPH FOR THE MOON IS THE SEMI-CIRCLE OR CRESCENT. It is a symbol for the receptiveness of the soul and is associated with feminine energies and the ebb and flow of the rhythms of life. In some Islamic traditions it represents the gateway to paradise and the realms of bliss.

The Sun and Moon are the two complementary poles of your personality, like yang and yin, masculine and feminine, active and reflective, career and home, father and mother. The Moon comes into its own as a guide at night, the time of sleeping consciousness. It also has a powerful effect on the waters of the earth. Likewise, the Moon in your birth chart describes what you respond to instinctively and feel 'in your waters', often just below the level of consciousness. It is your private radar system, sending you messages via your body responses and feelings, telling you whether a situation seems safe or scary, nice or nasty. Feelings provide vital information about circumstances in and around you. Ignore them at your peril; that will lead you into emotional, and sometimes even physical, danger. Eating disorders tend to be associated with being out of touch with, or neglecting, the instincts and the body, both of which the Moon describes.

Extraordinary though it might seem to those who are emotionally tuned in, some people have great difficulty in knowing what they are feeling. One simple way is to pay attention to your body. Notice any sensations that attract your attention. Those are linked to your feelings. Now get a sense of whether they are pleasant or unpleasant, then try to put a more exact name to what those feelings might be. Is it sadness, happiness, fear? What is it that they are trying to tell you? Your Moon hints at what will strongly activate your feelings. Learning to trust and decode this information will help make the world seem – and be – a safer place.

The Moon represents your drive to nurture and protect yourself and others. Its sign, house and aspects describe how you respond and adapt emotionally to situations and what feeds you, in every sense of the word. It gives information about your home and home life and how you experienced your mother, family and childhood, as well as describing your comfort zone of what feels familiar – the words 'family' and 'familiar' come from the same source. It shows, too, what makes you feel secure and what could comfort you when you're feeling anxious. Your Moon describes what moves and motivates you powerfully at the deepest instinctual level and indicates what is truly the 'matter' in – or with – your life.

Knowing children's Moon signs can help parents and teachers better understand their insecurities and respect their emotional make-up and needs, and so prevent unnecessary hurt, or even harm, to sensitive young lives. It's all too easy to expect that our children and parents should have the same emotional wiring as we do, but that's rarely how life works. Finding our parents' Moon signs can be a real revelation. It can often help us understand where they are coming from, what they need and why they react to us in the way they do. Many of my clients have been able to find the understanding and compassion to forgive their parents when they realised that they were doing their very best with the emotional resources available to them.

In relationships it is important that your Moon's requirements are met to a good enough extent. For example, if you have your Moon in Sagittarius you must have adventure, freedom and the opportunity to express your beliefs. If being with your partner constantly violates these basic needs, you will never feel secure and loved and the relationship could, in the long term, undermine you. However, if your Moon feels too comfortable, you will never change and grow. The art is to get a good working balance between support and challenge.

A man's Moon sign can show some of the qualities he will unconsciously select in a wife or partner. Some of the others are shown in his Venus sign. Many women can seem much more like their Moon signs than their Sun signs, especially if they are involved in mothering a family and being a support system for their husbands or partners. It is only at the mid-life crisis that many women start to identify more with the qualities of their own Suns rather than living that out through their partners' ambitions. Similarly, men tend to live out the characteristics of their Moon signs through their wives and partners until mid-life, often quite cut off from their own feelings and emotional responses. If a man doesn't seem at all like his Moon sign, then check out the women in his life. There's a good chance that his wife, mother or daughter will show these qualities.

Your Moon can be in any sign, including the same one as your Sun. Each sign belongs to one of the four elements: Fire, Earth, Air or Water. The element of your Moon can give you a general idea of how you respond to new situations and what you need to feel safe and comforted. We all become anxious if our Moon's needs are not being recognised and attended to. We then, automatically, go into our personal little rituals for making ourselves feel better. Whenever you are feeling distressed, especially when you are way out of your comfort zone in an unfamiliar situation, do something to feed and soothe your Moon. You're almost certain to calm down quickly.

Fire Moons

If you have a fire Moon in Aries, Leo or Sagittarius, your first response to any situation is to investigate in your imagination the possibilities for drama, excitement and self-expression. Feeling trapped by dreary routine in an ordinary humdrum life crushes you completely. Knowing that you are carrying out a special mission feeds your soul. To you, all the world's a stage and a voyage of discovery. Unless you are at the centre of the action playing some meaningful role, anxiety and depression can set in. To feel secure, you have to have an appropriate outlet for expressing your spontaneity, honourable instincts and passionate need to be of unique significance. The acknowledgement, appreciation and feedback of people around you are essential, or you don't feel real. Not to be seen and appreciated, or to be overlooked, can feel like a threat to your very existence.

Earth Moons

If you have an earth Moon in Taurus, Virgo or Capricorn, you'll respond to new situations cautiously and practically. Rapidly changing circumstances where you feel swept along and out of control are hard for you to cope with. You need time for impressions to sink in. Sometimes it is only much later, after an event has taken place, that you become sure what you felt about it. Your security lies in slowing down, following familiar routines and rituals, even if they are a bit obsessive, and focusing on something, preferably material – possibly the body itself or nature – which is comforting because it is still there. Indulging the senses in some way often helps too, through food, sex or body care. So does taking charge of the practicalities of the immediate situation, even if this is only mixing the drinks or passing out clipboards. To feel secure, you need continuity and a sense that you have your hand on the rudder of your own life. Think of the rather irreverent joke about the man seeming to cross himself in a crisis, all the while actually touching his most valued possessions to check that they are still intact – spectacles, testicles, wallet and watch. That must have been thought up by someone with the Moon in an earth sign.

Air Moons

When your Moon is in an air sign – Gemini, Libra or Aquarius – you feel most secure when you can stand back from situations and observe them from a distance. Too much intimacy chokes you and you'll tend to escape it by going into your head to the safety of ideas and analysis. Even in close relationships you need your mental, and preferably physical, space. You often have to think, talk or write about what you are feeling before you are sure what your feelings are. By putting them 'out there' so that you can examine them clearly, you can claim them as your own. Unfairness and unethical behaviour can upset you badly and make you feel uneasy until you have done something about it or responded in some way. It can be easy with an air Moon to be unaware of, or to ignore, your own feelings because you are more responsive to ideas, people and situations outside of yourself that may seem to have little connection with you. This is not a good idea, as it cuts you off from the needs of your body as well as your own emotional intelligence. Making opportunities to talk, play with and exchange ideas and information can reduce the stress levels if anxiety strikes.

Water Moons

Finally, if your Moon is in a water sign – Cancer, Scorpio or Pisces – you are ultra-sensitive to atmospheres, and you can experience other people's pain or distress as if they were your own. You tend to take everything personally and, even if the situation has nothing at all to do with you, feel responsible for making it better. Your worst nightmare is to feel no emotional response coming back from other people. That activates your deep-seated terror of abandonment, which can make you feel that you don't exist and is, quite literally, what you fear even more than death. If you feel insecure, you may be tempted to resort to emotional manipulation to try to force intimacy with others – not a good idea, as this can lead to the very rejection that you dread. You are at your most secure when the emotional climate is positive and you have trusted, supportive folk around who will winkle you out of hiding if you become too reclusive. With a water Moon, it is vital to learn to value your own feelings and to take them seriously – and to have a safe, private place you can retreat to when you feel emotionally fragile. As you never forget anything which has made a feeling impression on you, sometimes your reactions are triggered by unconscious memories of things long past, rather than what is taking place in the present. When you learn to interpret them correctly, your feelings are your finest ally and will serve you well.

Finding Your Moon Sign

If you don't yet know your Moon sign, before looking it up, you could have some fun reading through the descriptions that follow and seeing if you can guess which one it is. To find your Moon sign, check your year and date of birth in the tables on pp. 99–112. For a greater in-depth understanding of your Moon sign, you might like to read about its characteristics in the book in this series about that sign.

At the beginning of each section are the names of some well-known Leos with that particular Moon sign. You can find more about them in Chapter Ten.

Sun in Leo with Moon in Aries

Isabel Allende	Jacqueline Kennedy Onassis	Jennifer Lopez
José Silva	John Simpson	Andy Warhol

You live in a brightly coloured, fairy-tale world, with you as hero or heroine of the piece. Action and enterprise make you feel alive and you like to be at the forefront – and centre-stage – wherever there is a challenge to be taken or a conflict underway. BBC foreign affairs correspondent John Simpson has been referred to as an action addict. He caused more than a few raised eyebrows throughout the world as he strode confidently into Kabul amid a cheering crowd, commentating live, when the city fell, even before the conquering troops had entered and taken possession. There were other broadcasters inside Kabul, but being a Leo, guess who stole the spotlight? As visualisation is the first step in achievement, you can use your vivid imagination to help you take effective action in the outer world. José Silva has used this talent to develop Mind Control Method, which has helped countless individuals make better and more creative lives for themselves. You can be a first-class entrepreneur, as you tend to trust your hunches and have the confidence, which can sometimes verge on bare-faced cheek, to push your schemes through. One way or another, life around you is unlikely to be dull.

A few with an Aries Moon experience violence either against them or around them, as did Jacqueline Kennedy, whose husband was assassinated by her side, or Andy Warhol, who was shot at by a crazed fan. Fortunately this is not how this combination usually works! Your biggest challenge is to find a way of having your needs met without either being intimidated by life or bulldozing over other people's sensitivities. Achieve that balance and you combine the best of power and glory.

Sun in Leo with Moon in Taurus

Halle Berry	Max Bircher-Benner	Bill Clinton
Mick Jagger	Monica Lewinsky	George Bernard Shaw

With this combination the physical appetites are large and in some it can mean a powerful libido and a reluctance to stick to just one mate. Mick Jagger's long-suffering partner Jerry Hall finally hit him where it hurts a Taurus Moon most – in the bank balance – for a cool £15.5 million after he had one affair too many. For President Bill Clinton and Monica Lewinsky their earth Moons moved, but that was one performance that they would probably have preferred not to have had replayed for an audience of millions.

You need not, however, be run by your sexual passions. Having enough money could be your issue, or pampering your body or enjoying good food may be more your style. Irish playwright George Bernard Shaw was a strict vegetarian, on both compassionate and health grounds, but could frequently be seen shovelling great quantities of cake into his mouth like a child, whilst holding forth on learned topics. Your firmness of resolve can sometimes make you dogmatic and occasionally a bit of a control freak. Dr Max Bircher-Benner kept his patients on a strict regime in his natural health clinic. One day he found members of the Russian royal family breaking the rules by smoking, drinking and gambling and staying up late. Ignoring their rank, he threw them out on their ears and only allowed them back after they had grovelled and agreed to obey his orders to the letter. This they did, to the betterment of their health. Being in nature and slowing down enough to enjoy regular intervals of peace and quiet, watching the grass grow, helps to support your health and sense of well-being.

Sun in Leo with Moon in Gemini

| Amelia Earhart | Davy Crockett | Norris and Ross McWhirter |
| Clive Sinclair | Alfred, Lord Tennyson | Shelley Winters |

Fresh facts delight you, whether these are trivial pursuits or knowledge of a more substantial nature. This information you'll be bursting to share with others, preferably in a way that makes maximum impact. You don't just tell a story or pass on news; you dramatise or embellish it in some way, putting a colourful angle or spin on it, all the better to package it with. A Leo Sun's interest is in all that is biggest, greatest and best, while a Gemini Moon loves fascinating titbits of information so it's hardly surprising that *The Guinness Book of Records* was started by the McWhirter twins, who have just that combination.

You have a deep-seated need for frequent change and mental stimulation so it's not easy for you to concentrate your energies on just one person or project. You like to keep up with the latest trends in whatever fields interest you – and those are likely to be many. With your love of freedom, you can't bear to be tied down to too much routine. Being constantly on the move is more your style.

You've a healthy curiosity, that at times could border on downright nosiness, for all that's going on around you. With your inventive mind and skill at making connections, both social and intellectual, you are the best possible person to sell ideas, broker deals and arrange to link up like-minded people.

You have a way with words and when in love can write the most romantic poems and letters. Not being able or allowed to communicate is, for you, like having your oxygen supply cut off – so your phone, fax and email will rarely be idle.

Sun in Leo with Moon in Cancer

| Emily Brontë | Zelda Fitzgerald | Princess Margaret |
| Sean Penn | Roman Polanski | Mae West |

Until you understand that two of the most powerful parts of your personality want very different things, this is not generally the easiest mix to live with, but once you've cracked the combination, you are on to a winner. Your Moon makes you acutely sensitive to rejection and if you feel unwanted you could retreat into your familiar nest, pull the bedclothes over your head huffily and not put your nose out of the door for days on end. Yet your Sun loves to party and perform.

Powerfully intuitive, you can pick up on other people's feelings and often experience them as if they were your own – then start to act them out. As you have a sure feel for the sensationalism that appeals to people's basic instincts, you could succeed in working with the public, especially in the media. Emily Brontë's novel of passion and revenge, *Wuthering Heights*, is one of the most enduringly popular works of literature. It's important to take care who you allow into your circle of intimates, as you need to be cherished and protected as well as admired. You are at your best when surrounded by people who understand and adore you, who'll let you be alone when you're in one of your unreasonable strops, then welcome you back royally when you're fit for company.

Home life matters to you and you can make a wonderfully caring parent. If you were hurt or humiliated in childhood, though, you can detach from your feelings as self-protection, or even cut off from your family. You can be terribly touchy about slights, real or imagined, and are gifted at holding and nursing grudges. However, if the offending one apologises sincerely you can also forgive wholeheartedly and graciously.

Sun in Leo with Moon in Leo

Robert Graves	Peter O'Toole	Patrick Swayze
Shirley Williams	Barbara Windsor	Marion Woodman

With your charismatic and larger-than-life personality, you can draw the crowds and stop the show but, until you truly see that others are every bit as important as you are, you could also be rather self-centred. Many with this combination have an interest in mythology or tales of nobility, largely because it is how you see your own life – with you, in glorious, glowing Technicolor, filling the starring role. Robert Graves, apart from being considered the greatest love poet of his generation, was also the author of *Greek Myths*, which has become a classic. Jungian therapist and writer Marion Woodman uses myths and fairy tales to help her clients heal. A bit like Henry Higgins in *My Fair Lady*, you are often keen to help improve others, but it is always worth checking with those you're trying to sculpt into better shape that they share your vision about how and what they should become.

Whatever your failings, petty-mindedness is not one of them. Generosity pours out of you as naturally as sunshine on a summer's day. You are proud and dignified and intent on receiving the accolades and status that you know you deserve. It's important to you that you're noticed, and at the centre of an admiring crowd, so you'll rarely let yourself down by acting meanly, as you hate to be seen in a poor light. It's best not to let your judgement be clouded by flattery, and to resist the temptation to resort to tantrums when you don't get your own way. Depending on whether or not your ego dominates, you can be a must-to-avoid as a self-absorbed tyrant, or a force for great good, affecting many lives for the better.

Sun in Leo with Moon in Virgo

| Princess Anne | Dustin Hoffman | Trevor McDonald |
| Madonna | Robert Redford | J.K. Rowling |

You like things done properly, and with your critical eye and tongue, you can penetrate to the heart of any matter and spot flaws instantly. You won't tolerate anything less than the finest work performance either from yourself or from anyone associated with you. Dustin Hoffman and Madonna both have the reputation of being perfectionists, which doesn't always make life easy for work colleagues or assistants. It is, however, this attention to detail and steady working away at improving and honing their technique that has led to them being recognised as world-class stars and serious professionals.

You're not afraid of hard work; in fact, you thrive on it. Your sense of duty and need to be of service are likely to be strong. That, together with your executive and leadership skills, can mean that you can get things done and make a substantial contribution to the community. Princess Anne has the reputation of taking her duties seriously and being the most hard-working of all the royals. J.K. Rowling says that the conscientious swot, Hermione, whose expertise can be relied on to fix most problems, is based on – herself. You have a fine analytical mind and can express yourself clearly, while your interest in body care and health can sometimes make you a bit of a fusspot and hypochondriac. For you, only the best will do, but clothes, home and habits must be practical too and if the functional wins over the dramatic you could veer towards the dowdy. Much more likely, though, you'll have a wonderful sense of style, often favouring the 'less is more' approach, with a few dramatic splashes to highlight the effect.

Sun in Leo with Moon in Libra

| Madame Blavatsky | Fidel Castro | Julia Child |
| Rose Kennedy | Audrey Tatou | Louis Vuitton |

Confrontation and anger can upset you horribly and you will do almost anything to avoid them. On the other hand (one of your favourite phrases), being an idealist, injustice and unfairness motivates you to put your considerable talents and energy into doing something about it, rather like Audrey Tatou's character in *Amélie*, a sweetly innocent girl in Paris, with her own sense of justice, who decides to help those around her, with heart-warming consequences. Or like Fidel Castro, who runs Cuba as a benign dictator. You are wonderful at taking over and settling disputes, as you can see everyone's point of view. Getting your own way with the minimum of effort is easy. You simply charm others into believing it was their idea all along.

You are tuned in to the feelings of whoever you are with and sometimes neglect your own needs in the process. You're a natural peacemaker and your gracious manner puts people at their ease. Because you focus so much on others, they usually give you their full attention which, of course, makes your Leo Sun purr. With your appreciation of elegance and luxury, you do like the finer things in life. Work involving style and beauty could appeal – think Vuitton luggage, which conjures up visions of glamour and elegance. Your partner needs to be someone with whom you can share ideas and ideals, as well as being easy on the eye. As your view of life and relationships is romantic, and sometimes naive, you believe that the honeymoon phase should go on forever. You can be shocked and upset if people don't play the game. Preferring to keep things light,

when situations or people become too heavy you can feel
trapped and you're capable of engineering an elegant exit.

Sun in Leo with Moon in Scorpio

Ben Affleck	Jenny Bond	Alex Haley
Alfred Hitchcock	Stanley Kubrick	The Queen Mother

Because you feel so intensely, as a child you would have been
acutely aware of any secrets, emotional undercurrents and
subjects that were taboo in your household. You may,
unfortunately, also have witnessed or experienced the
misuse of power. One wonders what was behind Alfred
Hitchcock's remark that 'television has brought back
murder into the home – where it belongs'. As your
antennae are constantly set to monitor threats to you and
yours, you can spot corruption and when something is 'off'
instantly. At times you could be rather paranoid, but just
because you are paranoid it doesn't mean that nobody is
going to turn your shower into a bloodbath.

Being so aware of potential threats, you tend to hide
behind a smokescreen of secrecy and may even appear shy.
You guard your privacy fiercely and prefer people to know
about you only what you choose to give out. You are equally
skilled at taking the emotional temperature and
manoeuvring it to your own advantage to remove rivals and
enemies, or to expose corruption. You love to be in charge
and until everything and everyone around is under your
control you can feel insecure, so you could be a bit of a
dictator behind that affable, party-loving exterior.
Radiating charisma and restrained sexuality, you can seem
calm and unruffled on the surface yet, underneath, your
emotions can churn like a seething cauldron. Power, wealth

and the mysteries of sex, birth, death and betrayal have a fascination for you and will shape your destiny in some way, though hopefully not as dramatically as in the case of the Queen Mother. An intensely private person, her happy family life was ripped apart as she was thrust into the limelight as Queen after the political and sexual scandal of her brother-in-law's abdication.

Leo Sun with Moon in Sagittarius

| Neil Armstrong | Ray Bradbury | Geraldine Chaplin |
| T.E. Lawrence | Herman Melville | Martha Stewart |

A Moon in Sagittarius loves to travel and explore – and exploration doesn't come much bigger or further than the Moon. So who better than a Leo with a Sagittarius Moon to be first to set foot on it? Neil Armstrong's sense of drama did not desert him in his finest hour, either. He described that historic occasion as 'one small step for man, one giant leap for mankind' and then returned home to New York to a ticker-tape reception. You can be quite careless and even clumsy sometimes, but Sagittarius is also the sign of the lucky escape. Once, when Armstrong's jet trainer crashed, he parachuted to earth safely from 12,000 feet.

You can't keep a good Leo in a subordinate position. T.E. Lawrence was another of your kind not content to stay at home. He was a fairly junior soldier who became a self-appointed leader of the Arabs in their bid for freedom, well above his British Army station. Needless to say, this did not endear him to his senior officers. You're enormous fun to be around. With the soul of a gypsy, if you can't pack up your bags and wander, you are totally miserable. Unless there are some weightier aspects in your chart, responsibilities are anathema to you. Your sensors are highly attuned to people in need of your advice and wisdom. You love to teach and sometimes to preach, aiming to bring out the best in others, but you may need to take care not to slide into moral indignation or self-righteousness. You're a wonderful promoter and entrepreneur, trusting your hunches and happy to take a risk and a gamble. The fields of teaching, publishing and broadcasting could be very profitable for you.

Leo Sun with Moon in Capricorn

Lucille Ball	Napoleon Bonaparte	Gene Kelly
Yves St Laurent	Arnold Schwarzenegger	Norman Schwarzkopf

You are quick to respond to responsibilities, and have probably had to be dutiful from your early days. Family life may have been bleak, or strict and traditional. A Capricorn Moon often has an emotionally restricted childhood. This can be because the parents were poor, or elderly or overburdened, or you may have been expected to behave in certain ways that were dictated by others, rather than being allowed simply to be a spontaneous child. You may feel that love has to be earned, rather than simply flowing towards you just because you're you. Like all Leos, you are at your best in the leadership role but, unlike most other Leos, you are willing to put in the hard graft and apply the necessary self-discipline to get to the top.

Your worst nightmare is to be humiliated in public by being ticked off or made to look small. Prestige and rank and all the symbols of moving up the hierarchy are of the utmost importance to you. You want both recognition and social approval. At your very best, you have an invaluable contribution to make as a pillar of society. At worst, you can be a harsh, demanding and punishing despot. If you do find yourself acting like this, it may be because you received this kind of treatment yourself at home and need to learn that there are other, and better, ways of relating. Hard work makes you feel good, as does time on your own. It would be surprising if you didn't have occasional patches of dark depression, where you believe that nobody loves you. When this mood strikes, it's often best to dramatise your feelings, exaggerating them so much that you start to laugh at your gloom, and get yourself back on track.

Leo Sun with Moon in Aquarius

Rupert Brooke	Donald Dewar	Henry Ford
Melanie Griffith	Elsie Inglis	Jacqueline Susann

It's not always easy for you to know what you're feeling, as you can be much more tuned in to what needs attending to in society as a whole, rather than focusing on your own physical or emotional well-being. No matter how long you have been in your home, you may have a sense of impermanence, always waiting for the call to move on. Scotland's first First Minister, Donald Dewar, camped at his home among half-emptied packing cases and ate at supermarket canteens when he wasn't grazing off canapés at official receptions.

As you have a strong social conscience, you could be excellent at heading up a humanitarian organisation. You could equally well run an innovative business organisation, strong on teamwork. Taking up a position of command to bring about positive change in the community could suit you perfectly. This is what Elsie Inglis, one of Scotland's first women doctors, did. Appalled at male prejudice and lack of decent maternity facilities, she sidestepped the system and set up a maternity hospital with an all-female staff – and a medical school for women only too. A tiny nuclear family with doors firmly closed to the outside world is rarely for you. You are much more at home living as part of some kind of community; being with like-minded friends or participating in an ongoing internet group can give you a real sense of family. Your childhood may have been disrupted or unsettled, or your mother cool, detached and independent – or possibly eccentric or ahead of her time. Though you are probably more openly friendly and democratic than the average Leo, strong emotions and wall-to-wall intimacy can make you feel anxious, so freedom and time alone to do your own thing are essential.

Leo Sun with Moon in Pisces

| Coco Chanel | Mata Hari | P.D. James |
| V.S. Naipaul | Robert de Niro | Percy Bysshe Shelley |

You carry around with you an atmosphere of glamour and charisma or suffering and confusion – and possibly both. Deep down you may feel flawed and helpless, and being so sensitive you can experience the pain of the world as if it were your own. You respond powerfully to victims and can feel guilty, edgy and responsible until you have done something to aid their plight. With your instinctive need to serve others, and not just yourself, you love to rescue the less fortunate and, through this, can come to know your own nobility. One man with this combination describes himself as a hero – to wounded women, he adds with a rueful smile.

You may have idealised your parents – or suffered in early life by feeling, or even being, abandoned because they were, for some reason, unavailable to look after you in the way you yearned for. Coco Chanel was sent to an orphanage at the age of 12 and never saw her father again. Because of your vulnerability, your feelings are easily bruised. To cope, some people become cynical and tough to shut out what can seem like unbearable exposure to pain. You need to retreat from the harshness and limitations of everyday life from time to time. Be careful with mind-altering substances like alcohol and chocolate, as you develop addictions easily. Music, spirituality or even just daydreaming is preferable. Your highest task is to bring the beauty and the love of heaven to earth in some dramatic way. Though you may not have the breathtakingly elegant fashion sense of Coco Chanel, or write exquisite poetry like Shelley, you can heal society's helpless, hurt and outcast with your compassionate acceptance.

EIGHT

Mercury – It's All in the Mind

☿ THE GLYPHS FOR THE PLANETS ARE MADE UP OF THREE SYMBOLS: the circle, the semi-circle and the cross. Mercury is the only planet, apart from Pluto, whose glyph is made up of all three of these symbols. At the bottom there is the cross, representing the material world; at the top is the semi-circle of the crescent Moon, symbolising the personal soul; and in the middle, linking these two, is the circle of eternity, expressed through the individual. In mythology, Mercury was the only god who had access to all three worlds – the underworld, the middle world of earth and the higher world of the gods. Mercury in your chart represents your ability, through your thoughts and words, to make connections between the inner world of your mind and emotions, the outer world of other people and events, and the higher world of intuition. Your Mercury sign can give you a great deal of information about the way your mind works and about your interests, communication skills and your preferred learning style.

It can be frustrating when we just can't get through to some people and it's easy to dismiss them as being either completely thick or deliberately obstructive. Chances are they are neither. It may be that you're simply not talking each other's languages. Knowing your own and other people's communication styles can lead to major breakthroughs in relationships.

Information about children's natural learning patterns can help us teach them more effectively. It's impossible to learn properly if the material isn't presented in a way that resonates with the way your mind works. You just can't 'hear' it, pick it up or grasp it. Wires then get crossed and the data simply isn't processed. Many children are seriously disadvantaged if learning materials and environments don't speak to them. You may even have been a child like that yourself. If so, you could easily have been left with the false impression that you are a poor learner just because you couldn't get a handle on the lessons being taught. Identifying your own learning style can be like finding the hidden key to the treasure room of knowledge.

The signs of the zodiac are divided into four groups by element:

> The fire signs: Aries, Leo and Sagittarius
> The earth signs: Taurus, Virgo and Capricorn
> The air signs: Gemini, Libra and Aquarius
> The water signs: Cancer, Scorpio and Pisces

Your Mercury will therefore belong to one of the four elements, depending on which sign it is in. Your Mercury can only be in one of three signs – the same sign as your Sun, the one before or the one after. This means that each sign has one learning style that is never natural to it. For Leo, this is the air style.

Mercury in each of the elements has a distinctive way of

operating. I've given the following names to the learning and communicating styles of Mercury through the elements. Mercury in fire – active imaginative; Mercury in earth – practical; Mercury in air – logical; and Mercury in water – impressionable.

Mercury in Fire: Active Imaginative

Your mind is wide open to the excitement of fresh ideas. It responds to action and to the creative possibilities of new situations. Drama, games and storytelling are excellent ways for you to learn. You love to have fun and play with ideas. Any material to be learned has to have some significance for you personally, or add to your self-esteem, otherwise you rapidly lose interest. You learn by acting out the new information, either physically or in your imagination. The most efficient way of succeeding in any goal is to make first a mental picture of your having achieved it. This is called mental rehearsal and is used by many top sportsmen and women as a technique to help improve their performance. You do this spontaneously, as your imagination is your greatest mental asset. You can run through future scenarios in your mind's eye and see, instantly, where a particular piece of information or situation could lead and spot possibilities that other people couldn't even begin to dream of. You are brilliant at coming up with flashes of inspiration for creative breakthroughs and crisis management.

Mercury in Earth: Practical

Endless presentations of feelings, theories and possibilities can make your eyes glaze over and your brain ache to shut down. What really turns you on is trying out these theories and possibilities to see if they work in practice. If they don't, you'll tend to classify them 'of no further interest'.

Emotionally charged information is at best a puzzling non-starter and at worst an irritating turn-off. Practical demonstrations, tried and tested facts and working models fascinate you. Hands-on learning, where you can see how a process functions from start to finish, especially if it leads to some useful material end-product, is right up your street. It's important to allow yourself plenty of time when you are learning, writing or thinking out what to say, otherwise you can feel rushed and out of control, never pleasant sensations for earth signs. Your special skill is in coming up with effective solutions to practical problems and in formulating long-range plans that bring concrete, measurable results.

Mercury in Air: Logical

You love learning about, and playing with, ideas, theories and principles. Often you do this best by arguing or bouncing ideas off other people, or by writing down your thoughts. Your special gift is in your ability to stand back and work out the patterns of relationship between people or things. You much prefer it when facts are presented to you logically and unemotionally and have very little time for the irrational, uncertainty or for personal opinions. You do, though, tend to have plenty of those kinds of views yourself, only you call them logical conclusions. Whether a fact is useful or not is less important than whether it fits into your mental map of how the world operates. If facts don't fit in, you'll either ignore them, find a way of making them fit, or, occasionally, make a grand leap to a new, upgraded theory. Yours is the mind of the scientist or chess player. You make a brilliant planner because you can be detached enough to take an overview of the entire situation.

Mercury in Water: Impressionable

Your mind is sensitive to atmospheres and emotional undertones and to the context in which information is presented. Plain facts and figures can often leave you cold and even intimidated. You can take things too personally and read between the lines for what you believe is really being said or taught. If you don't feel emotionally safe, you can be cautious about revealing your true thoughts. It may be hard, or even impossible, for you to learn properly in what you sense is a hostile environment. You are excellent at impression management. Like a skilful artist painting a picture, you can influence others to think what you'd like them to by using suggestive gestures or pauses and intonations. People with Mercury in water signs are often seriously disadvantaged by left-brain schooling methods that are too rigidly structured for them. You take in information best through pictures or images, so that you get a 'feel' for the material and can make an emotional bond with it, in the same way you connect with people. In emotionally supportive situations where there is a rapport between you and your instructors, or your learning material, you are able just to drink in and absorb circulating knowledge without conscious effort, sometimes not even being clear about how or why you know certain things.

Finding Your Mercury Sign

If you don't yet know your Mercury sign, you might like to see if you can guess what it is from the descriptions below before checking it out in the tables on pp. 113–15.

Sun in Leo with Mercury in Cancer

Alexandre Dumas	P.D. James	C.G. Jung
George Bernard Shaw	Martha Stewart	Alfred, Lord Tennyson

This is the least common Mercury sign to have if your Sun is in Leo and it can add a strong inward-looking dimension to your personality. You learn best when you have established some kind of emotional bond with the information to be assimilated and with any teacher who instructs you. Cold facts alone can feel unappealing and even alien. Your thoughts and words are strongly coloured by your emotions. Sometimes this can lead you to take everything too personally and leave you unable or unwilling to take a detached enough view to see the truth of the matter. It's hard for you to listen or put yourself across clearly if you are emotionally upset or feel that you have been put down, ignored or rejected in some way.

Once you have learned to set aside pride and touchiness, you can communicate your feelings skilfully and use your thoughts to analyse your feelings. The Swiss psychiatrist Jung used to have explosive outbursts of anger – not a particularly uncommon phenomenon for a Leo. But when the fire had died down, he would say to the shaken recipient, 'Now let's see what that was all about' and reflect carefully on the matter, coming up with valuable insights about himself and his relationship with the situation. You can do the same. This is an excellent combination for a writer, as you have a vivid imagination and a love of history, plus the ability to get under the skin of your characters and understand them from the inside, producing larger-than-life heroes that appeal to the popular imagination – like Alexandre Dumas' loveable *The Three Musketeers* or P.D. James's poetry-writing Inspector Dalgleish.

Sun in Leo with Mercury in Leo

Emily Brontë	Napoleon Bonaparte	Bill Clinton
Mick Jagger	Jacqueline Kennedy Onassis	Danielle Steele

As you have an ear for dramatic dialogue and an instinctive sense of timing, you know how to keep your audience in suspense. This can make you an actor, on or off a stage, a teller of enthralling tales or a writer of unputdownable page-turners. Even if you are not a creative writer or artist, you have the gift of knowing how to present your words to great effect. It's hard sometimes to resist the temptation to embellish or spin a good yarn. One man with this combination told me how he chased after and stopped a runaway car that was careering down a hill and about to mow down a pram containing a new-born baby. He had indeed applied a handbrake to a neglectfully parked vehicle. The rest was his story . . .

One junior employee I know leaves new acquaintances with the lasting impression that he is a high-ranking official with the ear of the president. He adds deprecating little asides like 'Of course, in my lowly station . . .' then smiles knowingly at his extended fingernails, leaving his audience thinking 'What a wonderful person, and so modest, too.' Most of your thoughts revolve around your own concerns and how you appear to others, so you are skilled at bringing the topic of conversation back to the main theme – you. You certainly don't like being spoken down to and will make your displeasure felt in no uncertain terms. On the up side, your stirring and dramatic manner of expressing yourself can make you a natural leader and promoter. If you hitch your wagon to an ideal bigger than your own ego, you can inspire yourself and others to live out the finest qualities of human nobility with triumph and honour.

Sun in Leo with Mercury in Virgo

Lucille Ball	Aubrey Beardsley	Jonathan Dimbleby
Ted Hughes	Barbara Windsor	Mae West

Details interest you. Your goal in learning, teaching and communicating is excellence, and that excellence is achieved by paying attention to every particular, discriminating and making choices at every turn, each one of which affects the finished product. Sloppiness irritates you and you can be critical and sometimes rather sharp with yourself – and with others who don't live up to your own exacting standards. Leo writers with this combination are usually skilled craftsmen and women, honing their words to a smoothly polished patina, with no trace of flab in their sentences. More than likely, you are quick-witted and clever with words. Some of Mae West's one-liners live on to give enjoyment to this day, such as 'Is that a gun in your pocket, or are you just glad to see me?' and 'It's not the men in my life that counts – it's the life in my men.' You are good at distilling the essence of a situation, stripping away all that is irrelevant and then saying it like it is, to excellent dramatic effect.

If you can't see how information can be put to some good practical purpose, it's unlikely to hold your attention for long. You enjoy ordering your data in neat, well-connected flow charts and like to make lists, then tick off each item as you have dealt with them. With your eye and ear for practical detail, you are more at home in the material world than most other Leos. Facts fascinate you and you are clever at putting them over in a way that entertains and informs. As well being a skilful TV and radio presenter, Jonathan Dimbleby has written well-researched biographies of both his father, the legendary Richard, and Prince Charles.

NINE

Venus – At Your Pleasure

♀ THE GLYPH FOR VENUS IS MADE UP OF THE CIRCLE OF ETERNITY on top of the cross of matter. Esoterically this represents love, which is a quality of the divine, revealed on earth through personal choice. The saying 'One man's meat is another man's poison' couldn't be more relevant when it comes to what we love. It is a mystery why we find one thing attractive and another unattractive, or even repulsive. Looking at the sign, aspects and house of your Venus can't give any explanation of this mystery, but it can give some clear indications of what it is that you value and find desirable. This can be quite different from what current fashion tells you you should like. For example, many people are strongly turned on by voluptuous bodies but the media constantly shows images of near-anorexics as the desirable ideal. If you ignore what you, personally, find beautiful and try to be, or to love, what at heart leaves you cold, you are setting yourself up for unnecessary pain and dissatisfaction. Being true to your Venus sign, even if other people think you are strange, brings joy and pleasure. It also builds up your self-esteem because it grounds you solidly in your own personal values. This, in turn, makes you much more attractive to others. Not only that, it improves your relationships immeasurably, because you are living authentically and not betraying yourself by trying to prove your worth to others by being something you are not.

Glittering Venus, the brightest planet in the heavens, was named after the goddess of love, war and victory. Earlier names for her were Aphrodite, Innana and Ishtar. She was beautiful, self-willed and self-indulgent but was also skilled in all the arts of civilisation.

Your Venus sign shows what you desire and would like to possess, not only in relationships but also in all aspects of your taste, from clothes and culture to hobbies and hobby-horses. It identifies how and where you can be charming and seductive and skilful at creating your own type of beauty yourself. It also describes your style of attracting partners and the kind of people that turn you on. When your Venus is activated you feel powerful, desirable and wonderfully, wickedly indulged and indulgent. When it is not, even if someone has all the right credentials to make a good match, the relationship will always lack that certain something. If you don't take the chance to express your Venus to a good enough degree somewhere in your life, you miss out woefully on delight and happiness.

Morning Star, Evening Star

Venus appears in the sky either in the morning or in the evening. The ancients launched their attacks when Venus became a morning star, believing that she was then in her warrior-goddess role, releasing aggressive energy for victory in battle. If you're a morning-star person, you're likely to be impulsive, self-willed and idealistic, prepared to hold out until you find the partner who is just right for you.

Relationships and business dealings of morning-star Venus people are said to prosper best whenever Venus in the sky is a morning star. If you are an early bird, you can check this out. At these times Venus can be seen in the eastern sky before the Sun has risen.

The name for Venus as an evening star is Hesperus and it was then, traditionally, said to be sacred to lovers. Evening-star people tend to be easy-going and are open to negotiation, conciliation and making peace. If you are an evening-star Venus person, your best times in relationship and business affairs are said to be when Venus can be seen, jewel-like, in the western sky after the Sun has set.

Because the orbit of Venus is so close to the Sun, your Venus can only be in one of five signs. You have a morning-star Venus if your Venus is in one of the two signs that come before your Sun sign in the zodiac. You have an evening-star Venus if your Venus is in either of the two signs that follow your Sun sign. If you have Venus in the same sign as your Sun, you could be either, depending on whether your Venus is ahead of or behind your Sun. (You can find out which at the author's website www.janeridderpatrick.com.)

If you don't yet know your Venus sign, you might like to read through all of the following descriptions and see if you can guess what it is. You can find out for sure on pp. 116–18.

At the beginning of each section are the names of some well-known Leos with that particular Venus sign. You can find out more about them in Chapter Ten, Famous Leo Birthdays.

Sun in Leo with Venus in Gemini

Clara Bow	Sandra Bullock	Amelia Earhart
Jacqueline Kennedy Onassis	Ira Progoff	Alfred, Lord Tennyson

You're drawn to intelligent, sharp-witted partners with a clever sense of humour. As you're friendly yet curious and detached, you need a lot of freedom. Being tied down to one person or career could be difficult for you, as you usually prefer to keep your options open, or even to have several irons in the fire at one time. In a letter to her future husband, aviator Amelia Earhart wrote that she would not hold him, or herself, to any medieval code of faithfulness, saying that she couldn't guarantee to endure forever the confinements of even an attractive cage. Actress Clara Bow was a red-hot tootsie with more lovers than most of us could ever imagine, and fan mail to match. Alternatively, like Jacqueline Kennedy, you could be attracted to partners with ants in their pants. You'd quickly become bored with someone too predictable. This combination, however, doesn't always come out in a varied and interesting sex life. You may instead be passionate about intellectual affairs, socialising and communicating. Ira Progoff devised a type of self-therapy that involves keeping voluminous notes about your own life and affairs, romantic or otherwise, while Tennyson used to store screeds of poetry in his head and had to be coaxed to actually write it down.

With your finger on the pulse of all the latest gossip, you're usually delightful company, flirtatious and charming, and can't wait to be seen at all the newest trendy places, the classier the better. As communication with your partner is essential, your phone bill could be ruinous and when romantically inclined you can write the most deliciously passionate love letters.

Sun in Leo with Venus in Cancer

Ben Affleck	Kate Bush	Jerry Garcia
Dustin Hoffman	C.G. Jung	The Queen Mother

Whether you're a man or a woman, you've a soft, caring feminine side. Childhood memories often have a far-reaching effect on your later life and can help shape your choice of partner, as well as your career. In his book *Memories, Dreams, Reflections* (all words associated with the sign of Cancer), Swiss psychologist C.G. Jung recalls clearly, as an old man, powerful emotional events that laid the foundation for his work, which changed the face of twentieth-century psychology. Even musician Jerry Garcia of The Grateful Dead, a hard-living, drugs-and-booze party animal, wrote a book about his own childhood memories, full of photographs of old faces and places.

You're fiercely loyal to home, family and, often, your native land. You love and cherish your nearest and dearest, and will protect and accept them no matter what they do. It's important for you to feel needed. So is building a secure nest as a refuge from the world outside, as, for you, home is where your heart beats happiest. You enjoy all that's comfortable, beautiful and luxurious and can be quite self-indulgent. Venus in Cancer adds sensitivity, and a tendency to touchiness – sometimes even childishness – to your proud Leo Sun. Although financial and domestic security is so vitally important, you may have a rather extravagant streak too. You like to mother, or be mothered by, your partner and could be rather more clingy and vulnerable than you care to admit. You want to be petted, cherished and admired for your good qualities but can sometimes be taken advantage of because of your willingness to oblige. Learning to listen to, value, respect and appreciate your feelings and intuitions, however odd they seem at times, will lead to increased wisdom and bring you great pleasure.

Sun in Leo with Venus in Leo

| Diamond Jim Brady | Coco Chanel | Whitney Houston |
| Monica Lewinsky | Madonna | Andy Warhol |

For you, the bigger and more glamorous the better. You may not be as flashy as Diamond Jim Brady, the American super salesman and railway tycoon who entertained lavishly, gave recklessly and amassed an eye-popping collection of diamonds, but you would have to have some heavily restraining factors in you chart if you don't love to party and make a splash. One thing is sure – no way are you going to be overlooked. Full of fun, and sometimes full of yourself in equal measure, you're the belle of the ball and star of the show and you love entertaining in the grand manner or being lionised socially.

This is a wonderful placement for the performing arts or the world of fashion. You're in love with life, and with love, and have an impeccable flair for dramatic timing and presentation. Madonna has built a career on flamboyant and entertaining self-promotion. Being warm-hearted, romantic and affectionate, you love to pamper and spoil the people you love, but you do expect obedience in return. If you feel you've been slighted or overlooked, your pride can make you rather imperious. With your urge to impress, you may choose partners that you can be proud of and who make you look good by association. You're also attracted to people whose adulation could help shore up your ego and who give you unconditional love, admiration and tireless support. Dramatic and exciting courtship is what you adore, from opulent bouquets after the first meeting, right through to the fairy-tale happy-ever-after. Unless things go badly wrong, once committed to a relationship or project, you'll throw yourself into it heart and soul and stay there, loyally.

Sun in Leo with Venus in Virgo

Louis Armstrong	Julia Child	Mick Jagger
J.K. Rowling	Martha Stewart	Sir Roy Strong

Whatever you do has to be done properly and you like to get the details right, whether it is finely crafted writing or virtuoso performing, like jazz trumpeter Louis Armstrong. So many people wanted to copy his style that he kept a handkerchief over his hands while playing certain pieces. The success of Julia Child, author of the bestseller *The Art of French Cooking*, is in giving precise details of each minute step to be taken to produce cookery masterpieces simply, and with style.

You can be quite self-contained and there's a paradox at the heart of your personality. Part of you is sensual and highly sexed; another part is almost clinically fastidious, both in dress and personal hygiene, and would prefer to scrub up well before, and after, diving between the sheets. The challenge is to find a way of integrating both in your life. You yearn for romance and perfection in the one you love and you may prefer to have a partner who works away quietly in the background while you take the lion's share of attention. You do need, though, to be careful not to harp on about petty details. You can be quite fussy and nit-picking about your partner's shortcomings, as well as about your own. Learning tolerance may be quite a challenge but could improve your relationships dramatically. If you feel hurt, your criticism can be destructive but if you use your fine discrimination to analyse difficulties that inevitably arise in any relationship, you can make it work more smoothly. You love to serve, and your highest fulfilment often comes from being useful to others and helping change people's lives for the better, especially in practical ways.

Sun in Leo with Venus in Libra

Madame Blavatsky	Bill Clinton	Ted Hughes
Princess Margaret	Kenny Rogers	Shelley Winters

You've a powerful need to be seen as fair-minded and to be liked, admired – and obeyed. Harmony, marriage and all social relationships mean a lot to you. It can be hard for you to function without a partner. Men with this combination often feel more comfortable in the company of women, and vice versa. With your love of beauty, luxury and intellectual stimulation, you probably entertain elegantly and with quiet ostentation. Even if you're not good-looking – which is unlikely – you'll exude an air of attractiveness. You'd prefer your partner to be well-groomed and easy on the eye too. You're a stylish lover, and like the full works in romance – flowers, candlelit dinners, cigars . . .

Libra is the sign of the diplomat, architect, judge and general. Combining that with Leo Sun's ease of command makes you a formidable strategist. You're good at getting your own way. You can stand back, see what everybody wants and, quietly and without fuss, find a solution that suits everyone best, especially you. It's hard to out-manoeuvre you because you've thought through every move and objection and come up with a solution in advance. One problem that could arise, though, is that, because you dislike open confrontation so much, you're apt to be over-tolerant. In some situations it's better to step in and nip the problem in the bud, instead of hoping that all will be well if you are nice to everyone. Nothing, however, upsets you more than injustice and unfairness and you'll go to great lengths to put the balance right, usually charmingly and tactfully without ruffling too many feathers – though you'll do the latter if you have to.

TEN

Famous Leo Birthdays

FIND OUT WHO SHARES YOUR MOON, MERCURY AND VENUS SIGNS, and any challenging Sun aspects, and see what they have done with the material they were born with. Notice how often it is not just the personalities of the people themselves but the roles of actors, characters of authors and works of artists that reflect their astrological make-up. In reading standard biographies, I've been constantly astounded – and, of course, delighted – at how often phrases used to describe individuals could have been lifted straight from their astrological profiles. Check it out yourself!

A few people below have been given a choice of two Moons. This is because the Moon changed sign on the day that they were born and no birth time was available. You may be able to guess which one is correct if you read the descriptions of the Moon signs in Chapter Seven.

23 July
1888 Raymond Chandler, thriller writer, creator of private eye Philip Marlowe
Sun aspects: Saturn
Moon: Aquarius   Mercury: Cancer   Venus: Leo

24 July
1897 Amelia Earhart, pioneer aviator and first woman to fly across the Atlantic
Sun aspects: none
Moon: Gemini   Mercury: Leo   Venus: Gemini

25 July
1978 Louise Brown, the world's first test-tube baby
Sun aspects: Uranus
Moon: Aries   Mercury: Leo   Venus: Virgo

26 July
1875 Carl Gustav Jung, Swiss psychiatrist and mystic
Sun aspects: Neptune
Moon: Taurus   Mercury: Cancer   Venus: Cancer

27 July
1723 Sir Joshua Reynolds, one of the greatest portrait painters of all time
Sun aspects: Uranus
Moon: Gemini   Mercury: Cancer   Venus: Cancer

28 July
1929 Jacqueline Kennedy Onassis, elegant widow of US President John F. Kennedy
Sun aspects: none
Moon: Aries   Mercury: Leo   Venus: Gemini

29 July
1883 Benito Mussolini, Italian Fascist dictator, known as Il Duce (The Leader)
Sun aspects: none
Moon: Gemini   Mercury: Leo   Venus: Cancer

30 July
1863 Henry Ford, car manufacturer who developed the production line
Sun aspects: Pluto
Moon: Aquarius   Mercury: Leo   Venus: Virgo

31 July
1965 J.K. Rowling, bestselling author and creator of Harry Potter
Sun aspects: Neptune
Moon: Virgo   Mercury: Leo/Virgo   Venus: Virgo

1 August
1936 Yves Saint Laurent, couturier who pioneered ready-to-wear clothes
Sun aspects: Uranus
Moon: Capricorn   Mercury: Leo   Venus: Leo

2 August
1932 Peter O'Toole, charismatic Irish actor, *Lawrence of Arabia*
Sun aspects: Saturn
Moon: Leo   Mercury: Virgo   Venus: Cancer

3 August
1941 Martha Stewart, American homemaking entrepreneur
and TV personality
Sun aspects: Pluto
Moon: Sagittarius   Mercury: Cancer   Venus: Virgo

4 August
1900 Queen Elizabeth, the Queen Mother
Sun aspects: none
Moon: Scorpio   Mercury: Leo   Venus: Cancer

5 August
1930 Neil Armstrong, American astronaut and first man to
walk on the Moon
Sun aspects: none
Moon: Sagittarius   Mercury: Virgo   Venus: Virgo

6 August
1881 Sir Alexander Fleming, bacteriologist and discoverer
of penicillin
Sun aspects: Saturn, Neptune
Moon: Sagittarius   Mercury: Cancer   Venus: Gemini

7 August
1876 Mata Hari, exotic Dutch dancer, shot by the Germans
as a spy
Sun aspects: Uranus, Neptune, Pluto
Moon: Pisces   Mercury: Leo   Venus: Cancer

8 August
1937 Dustin Hoffman, American actor, *The Graduate*, *Rain
Man*
Sun aspects: Uranus
Moon: Virgo   Mercury: Virgo   Venus: Cancer

9 August
1963 Whitney Houston, singer, 'I Will Always Love You'
Sun aspects: Saturn, Neptune
Moon: Aries   Mercury: Virgo   Venus: Leo

10 August
1928 Eddie Fisher, singer, married to Debbie Reynolds then
Elizabeth Taylor
Sun aspects: none
Moon: Gemini   Mercury: Leo   Venus: Leo

11 August
1897 Enid Blyton, children's author, *Noddy in Toyland, The
Famous Five*
Sun aspects: Saturn, Uranus
Moon: Capricorn/Aquarius   Mercury: Virgo
Venus: Cancer

12 August
1881 Cecil B. de Mille, director of film spectaculars, *The
Ten Commandments*
Sun aspects: Saturn, Neptune, Pluto
Moon: Pisces   Mercury: Leo   Venus: Cancer

13 August
1899 Alfred Hitchcock, filmmaker and master of suspense,
Psycho, The Birds
Sun aspects: none
Moon: Scorpio   Mercury: Virgo   Venus: Leo

14 August
1947 Danielle Steele, American writer of over 50 bestselling romantic novels
Sun aspects: Saturn, Pluto
Moon: Cancer/Leo   Mercury: Leo   Venus: Leo

15 August
1771 Sir Walter Scott, prolific Scottish novelist, creator of the historical novel, *Ivanhoe*
Sun aspects: Saturn, Uranus
Moon: Libra/Scorpio   Mercury: Virgo   Venus: Leo

16 August
1958 Madonna, American superstar who frequently reinvents herself
Sun aspects: Pluto
Moon: Virgo   Mercury: Virgo   Venus: Leo

17 August
1892 Mae West, blonde American actress, quick with witty sexual innuendoes
Sun aspects: none
Moon: Cancer   Mercury: Virgo   Venus: Cancer

18 August
1937 Robert Redford, actor, *Butch Cassidy and the Sundance Kid*, *The Sting*
Sun aspects: none
Moon: Virgo   Mercury: Virgo   Venus: Virgo

19 August
1883 Coco Chanel, legendary glamorous French fashion designer
Sun aspects: Neptune, Pluto
Moon: Pisces   Mercury: Virgo   Venus: Leo

20 August
1918 Jacqueline Susann, self-promoting author of *The Valley of the Dolls*
Sun aspects: Saturn, Uranus
Moon: Aquarius   Mercury: Virgo   Venus: Leo

21 August
1930 Princess Margaret, once-glamorous, party-loving sister of Queen Elizabeth
Sun aspects: Neptune
Moon: Cancer   Mercury: Virgo   Venus: Libra

22 August
1867 Dr Max Bircher-Benner, Swiss doctor who pioneered natural healing.
Sun aspects: none
Moon: Taurus   Mercury: Leo   Venus: Leo

Other Leo people mentioned in this book
Ben Affleck, actor, *Good Will Hunting* ☆ Isabel Allende, Chilean author, *Eva Luna* ☆ Princess Anne, daughter of the Queen ☆ Louis Armstrong, jazz trumpeter ☆ John Logie Baird, inventor of television ☆ Lucille Ball, comedian, *I Love Lucy* ☆ Aubrey Beardsley, decadent illustrator, *Salome* ☆ Halle Berry, actress, *Die Another Day* ☆ Madame Blavatsky, founder of the Theosophical Society ☆ Napoleon Bonaparte, French emperor ☆ Jenny Bond, royal correspondent ☆ Clara Bow, actress and 1920s flapper ☆ Ray

Bradbury, science fiction writer, *The Martian Chronicles* ☆ Emily Brontë, author, *Wuthering Heights* ☆ Rupert Brooke, war poet, 'The Soldier' ☆ Sandra Bullock, actress, *28 Days* ☆ Kate Bush, singer, 'Wuthering Heights' ☆ Fidel Castro, Cuban dictator ☆ Geraldine Chaplin, actress, *Doctor Zhivago* ☆ Julia Child, cookery writer, *The Art of French Cooking* ☆ Bill Clinton, former US president ☆ Davy Crockett, American frontiersman ☆ Donald Dewar, Scotland's first First Minister ☆ Jonathan Dimbleby, broadcaster, *Newsnight*, *Any Questions* ☆ Alexandre Dumas, author, *The Count of Monte Cristo* ☆ Jerry Garcia, musician of The Grateful Dead ☆ Robert Graves, author and poet, *I, Claudius* ☆ Melanie Griffith, actress, *Working Girl* ☆ Alex Haley, author, *Roots* ☆ Ted Hughes, poet laureate, *Birthday Letters* ☆ Elsie Inglis, women's champion and medical pioneer ☆ Mick Jagger, lead singer of The Rolling Stones ☆ P.D. James, crime writer, *Unnatural Causes* ☆ David Koresh, psychopathic sect leader ☆ Stanley Kubrick, film maker, *A Clockwork Orange* ☆ T.E. Lawrence, Anglo-Irish soldier and arabist ☆ Monica Lewinsky, President Clinton's downfall ☆ Jennifer Lopez, actress, *Maid in Manhattan* ☆ Trevor McDonald, TV newsreader ☆ Norris and Ross McWhirter, twin creators of *The Guinness Book of Records* ☆ Herman Melville, author, *Moby Dick* ☆ Helen Mirren, actress, *Prime Suspect* ☆ V.S. Naipaul, author, *A House for Mr Biswas* ☆ Robert De Niro, actor, *Taxi Driver* ☆ Sean Penn, actor, *Dead Man Walking* ☆ Roman Polanski, film director, *Rosemary's Baby* ☆ Beatrix Potter, children's author, *Peter Rabbit* ☆ Ira Progoff, creator of intensive journal therapy ☆ Kenny Rogers, country and western singer, *Share Your Love* ☆ George Bernard Shaw, Irish author and playwright, *Pygmalion* ☆ Percy Bysshe Shelley, poet, 'Ozymandias' ☆ Arnold Schwarzenegger, actor, *The Terminator* ☆ Norman Schwarzkopf, Gulf War general, 'Stormin' Norman' ☆ José Silva, creator of the Silva Mind Technique ☆ John Simpson, BBC war correspondent ☆ Sir Roy Strong, flamboyant museum director ☆ Patrick

Swayze, actor, *Dirty Dancing* ☆ Audrey Tatou, French actress, *Amélie* ☆ Alfred, Lord Tennyson, poet, *The Lady of Shalott* ☆ Louis Vuitton, luxury luggage manufacturer ☆ Andy Warhol, artist, *Marilyn Monroe* ☆ Shirley Williams, politician and co-founder of the Social Democratic Party ☆ Barbara Windsor, bubbly actress in the *Carry On* series and *EastEnders* ☆ Shelley Winters, actress, *Alfie* ☆ Marion Woodman, Jungian therapist and author, *Addiction to Perfection*

ELEVEN

Finding Your Sun, Moon, Mercury and Venus Signs

ALL OF THE ASTROLOGICAL DATA IN THIS BOOK WAS CALCULATED by Astrolabe, who also supply a wide range of astrological software. I am most grateful for their help and generosity.

ASTROLABE, PO Box 1750, Brewster, MA 02631, USA www.alabe.com

PLEASE NOTE THAT ALL OF THE TIMES GIVEN ARE IN GREENWICH MEAN TIME (GMT). If you were born during British Summer Time (BST) you will need to subtract one hour from your birth time to convert it to GMT. If you were born outside of the British Isles, find the time zone of your place of birth and the number of hours it is different from GMT. Add the difference in hours if you were born west of the UK, and subtract the difference if you were born east of the UK to convert your birth time to GMT.

Your Sun Sign

Check your year of birth, and if you were born between the dates and times given the Sun was in Gemini when you were born – confirming that you're a Gemini. If you were born before the time on the date that Gemini begins in your year, you are a Taurean. If you were born after the time on the date Gemini ends in your year, you are a Cancerian.

Your Moon Sign

The Moon changes sign every two and a half days. To find your Moon sign, first find your year of birth. You will notice that in each year box there are three columns.

The second column shows the day of the month that the Moon changed sign, while the first column gives the abbreviation for the sign that the Moon entered on that date.

In the middle column, the month has been omitted, so that the dates run from, for example, 22 to 31 (July) and then from 1 to 23 (August).

In the third column, after the star, the time that the Moon changed sign on that day is given.

Look down the middle column of your year box to find your date of birth. If your birth date is given, look to the third column to find the time that the Moon changed sign. If you were born after that time, your Moon sign is given in the first column next to your birth date. If you were born before that time, your Moon sign is the one above the one next to your birth date.

If your birth date is not given, find the closest date before it. The sign shown next to that date is your Moon sign.

If you were born on a day that the Moon changed signs and you do not know your time of birth, try out both of that day's Moon signs and feel which one fits you best.

The abbreviations for the signs are as follows:

Aries – Ari   Taurus – Tau   Gemini – Gem   Cancer – Can
Leo – Leo   Virgo – Vir   Libra – Lib   Scorpio – Sco
Sagittarius – Sag   Capricorn – Cap   Aquarius – Aqu   Pisces – Pis

Your Mercury Sign

Find your year of birth and then the column in which your birthday falls. Look up to the top of the column to find your Mercury sign. You will see that some dates appear twice. This is because Mercury changed sign that day. If your birthday falls on one of these dates, try out both Mercury signs and see which one fits you best. If you know your birth time, you can find out for sure which Mercury sign is yours on my website – www.janeridderpatrick.com.

Your Venus Sign

Find your year of birth and then the column in which your birthday falls. Look up to the top of the column to find your Venus sign. Some dates have two possible signs. That's because Venus changed signs that day. Try them both out and see which fits you best. If the year you are interested in doesn't appear in the tables, or you have Venus in the same sign as your Sun and want to know whether you have a morning or evening star Venus, you can find the information on my website – www.janeridderpatrick.com.

♌ Leo Sun Tables ☉

YEAR	LEO BEGINS	LEO ENDS
1930	23 Jul 14.42	23 Aug 21.26
1931	23 Jul 20.21	24 Aug 03.10
1932	23 Jul 02.18	23 Aug 09.06
1933	23 Jul 08.05	23 Aug 14.52
1934	23 Jul 13.42	23 Aug 20.32
1935	23 Jul 19.32	24 Aug 02.23
1936	23 Jul 01.17	23 Aug 08.10
1937	23 Jul 07.06	23 Aug 13.57
1938	23 Jul 12.57	23 Aug 19.45
1939	23 Jul 18.36	24 Aug 01.31
1940	23 Jul 00.34	23 Aug 07.28
1941	23 Jul 06.26	23 Aug 13.16
1942	23 Jul 12.07	23 Aug 18.58
1943	23 Jul 18.04	24 Aug 00.54
1944	22 Jul 23.55	23 Aug 06.46
1945	23 Jul 05.45	23 Aug 18.26
1946	23 Jul 11.37	23 Aug 18.26
1947	23 Jul 17.14	24 Aug 00.08
1948	22 Jul 23.07	23 Aug 06.02
1949	23 Jul 04.56	23 Aug 11.48
1950	23 Jul 10.29	23 Aug 17.23
1951	23 Jul 16.20	23 Aug 23.16
1952	22 Jul 22.07	23 Aug 05.02
1953	23 Jul 03.52	23 Aug 10.45
1954	23 Jul 09.44	23 Aug 16.35
1955	23 Jul 15.24	23 Aug 22.18
1956	22 Jul 21.19	23 Aug 04.14
1957	23 Jul 03.14	23 Aug 10.07
1958	23 Jul 08.50	23 Aug 15.45
1959	23 Jul 14.45	23 Aug 21.43
1960	22 Jul 20.37	23 Aug 03.34
1961	23 Jul 02.23	23 Aug 09.18
1962	23 Jul 08.17	23 Aug 15.12
1963	23 Jul 13.59	23 Aug 20.57

YEAR	LEO BEGINS	LEO ENDS
1964	22 Jul 19.52	23 Aug 02.50
1965	23 Jul 01.48	23 Aug 08.42
1966	23 Jul 07.23	23 Aug 14.17
1967	23 Jul 13.15	23 Aug 20.12
1968	22 Jul 19.07	23 Aug 02.02
1969	23 Jul 00.48	23 Aug 07.43
1970	23 Jul 06.36	23 Aug 13.33
1971	23 Jul 12.14	23 Aug 19.15
1972	22 Jul 18.02	23 Aug 01.02
1973	22 Jul 23.55	23 Aug 06.53
1974	23 Jul 05.30	23 Aug 00.18
1975	23 Jul 11.21	23 Aug 18.23
1976	22 Jul 17.18	23 Aug 00.18
1977	22 Jul 23.03	23 Aug 06.00
1978	23 Jul 05.00	23 Aug 11.56
1979	23 Jul 10.48	23 Aug 17.46
1980	22 Jul 16.41	22 Aug 23.40
1981	22 Jul 22.39	23 Aug 05.38
1982	23 Jul 04.15	23 Aug 11.15
1983	23 Jul 10.04	23 Aug 17.07
1984	22 Jul 15.58	22 Aug 23.00
1985	22 Jul 21.36	23 Aug 04.35
1986	23 Jul 03.24	23 Aug 10.25
1987	23 Jul 09.06	23 Aug 16.09
1988	22 Jul 14.51	22 Aug 21.54
1989	22 Jul 20.45	23 Aug 03.46
1990	23 Jul 02.21	23 Aug 09.20
1991	23 Jul 08.11	23 Aug 15.12
1992	22 Jul 14.08	22 Aug 21.10
1993	22 Jul 19.50	23 Aug 02.50
1994	23 Jul 01.40	23 Aug 02.50
1995	23 Jul 07.29	23 Aug 14.34
1996	22 Jul 13.18	22 Aug 20.22
1997	22 Jul 19.15	23 Aug 02.19
1998	23 Jul 00.55	23 Aug 07.58
1999	23 Jul 06.44	23 Aug 13.51
2000	22 Jul 12.42	22 Aug 19.48

♌ Leo – Finding Your Moon Sign ☽

1930		
Can	23	*17:22
Leo	25	*17:18
Vir	27	*16:34
Lib	29	*17:18
Sco	31	*21:06
Sag	3	*04:24
Cap	5	*14:34
Aqu	8	*02:26
Pis	10	*15:02
Ari	13	*03:31
Tau	15	*14:37
Gem	17	*22:44
Can	20	*03:00
Leo	22	*03:57

1931		
Sco	22	*07:56
Sag	24	*12:19
Cap	26	*18:22
Aqu	29	*02:24
Pis	31	*12:46
Ari	3	*01:10
Tau	5	*14:04
Gem	8	*00:59
Can	10	*08:09
Leo	12	*11:29
Vir	14	*12:24
Lib	16	*12:45
Sco	18	*14:11
Sag	20	*17:46
Cap	22	*23:59

1932		
Ari	22	*20:52
Tau	25	*08:54
Gem	27	*21:25
Can	30	*08:06
Leo	1	*15:56
Vir	3	*21:14
Lib	6	*00:55
Sco	8	*03:49
Sag	10	*06:31
Cap	12	*09:38
Aqu	14	*13:54
Pis	16	*20:13
Ari	19	*05:18
Tau	21	*16:55

1933		
Leo	22	*17:18
Vir	25	*03:35
Lib	27	*11:43
Sco	29	*17:21
Sag	31	*20:26
Cap	2	*21:40
Aqu	4	*22:22
Pis	7	*00:11
Ari	9	*04:41
Tau	11	*12:45
Gem	13	*23:57
Can	16	*12:32
Leo	19	*00:21
Vir	21	*10:06

1934		
Sag	22	*06:27
Cap	24	*08:02
Aqu	26	*07:43
Pis	28	*07:20
Ari	30	*08:46
Tau	1	*13:26
Gem	3	*21:49
Can	6	*09:13
Leo	8	*22:07
Vir	11	*10:58
Lib	13	*22:32
Sco	16	*07:50
Sag	18	*14:10
Cap	20	*17:26
Aqu	22	*18:18

♌ Leo – Finding Your Moon Sign ☽

1935		
Tau	22	*21:21
Gem	25	*02:42
Can	27	*10:43
Leo	29	*21:04
Vir	1	*09:06
Lib	3	*21:54
Sco	6	*09:56
Sag	8	*19:24
Cap	11	*01:08
Aqu	13	*03:20
Pis	15	*03:18
Ari	17	*02:55
Tau	19	*04:08
Gem	21	*08:26

1936		
Lib	23	*17:30
Sco	26	*05:53
Sag	28	*17:55
Cap	31	*03:23
Aqu	2	*09:24
Pis	4	*12:35
Ari	6	*14:21
Tau	8	*16:11
Gem	10	*19:11
Can	12	*23:52
Leo	15	*06:20
Vir	17	*14:45
Lib	20	*01:17
Sco	22	*13:36

1937		
Aqu	23	*12:18
Pis	25	*20:20
Ari	28	*02:14
Tau	30	*06:31
Gem	1	*09:28
Can	3	*11:33
Leo	5	*13:35
Vir	7	*16:54
Lib	9	*22:59
Sco	12	*08:37
Sag	14	*20:58
Cap	17	*09:36
Aqu	19	*20:04
Pis	22	*03:27

1938		
Gem	22	*21:41
Can	24	*22:53
Leo	26	*22:25
Vir	28	*22:17
Lib	31	*00:36
Sco	2	*06:49
Sag	4	*17:01
Cap	7	*05:33
Aqu	9	*18:14
Pis	12	*05:44
Ari	14	*15:33
Tau	16	*23:24
Gem	19	*04:50
Can	21	*07:39

1939		
Sco	23	*12:05
Sag	25	*19:09
Cap	28	*04:50
Aqu	30	*16:14
Pis	2	*04:41
Ari	4	*17:22
Tau	7	*04:46
Gem	9	*13:04
Can	11	*17:20
Leo	13	*18:09
Vir	15	*17:19
Lib	17	*17:03
Sco	19	*19:20
Sag	22	*01:14

♌ Leo – Finding Your Moon Sign ☽

1940		
Pis	22	*01:58
Ari	24	*14:01
Tau	27	*02:55
Gem	29	*14:02
Can	31	*21:30
Leo	3	*01:19
Vir	5	*02:50
Lib	7	*03:49
Sco	9	*05:45
Sag	11	*09:29
Cap	13	*15:15
Aqu	15	*23:07
Pis	18	*09:10
Ari	20	*21:14

1941		
Leo	24	*05:47
Vir	26	*12:02
Lib	28	*16:40
Sco	30	*20:08
Sag	1	*22:49
Cap	4	*01:17
Aqu	6	*04:32
Pis	8	*09:51
Ari	10	*18:12
Tau	13	*05:32
Gem	15	*18:09
Can	18	*05:37
Leo	20	*14:14
Vir	22	*19:52

1942		
Sag	23	*11:57
Cap	25	*12:37
Aqu	27	*12:37
Pis	29	*13:49
Ari	31	*17:55
Tau	3	*01:48
Gem	5	*12:54
Can	8	*01:30
Leo	10	*13:38
Vir	13	*00:08
Lib	15	*08:30
Sco	17	*14:37
Sag	19	*18:34
Cap	21	*20:46

1943		
Tau	24	*03:53
Gem	26	*12:04
Can	28	*23:04
Leo	31	*11:43
Vir	3	*00:44
Lib	5	*12:50
Sco	7	*22:38
Sag	10	*05:07
Cap	12	*08:08
Aqu	14	*08:36
Pis	16	*08:06
Ari	18	*08:32
Tau	20	*11:40
Gem	22	*18:34

1944		
Vir	22	*22:24
Lib	25	*11:07
Sco	27	*23:15
Sag	30	*08:49
Cap	1	*14:41
Aqu	3	*17:09
Pis	5	*17:34
Ari	7	*17:43
Tau	9	*19:19
Gem	11	*23:39
Can	14	*07:03
Leo	16	*17:08
Vir	19	*05:00
Lib	21	*17:45

♌ Leo – Finding Your Moon Sign ☽

1945		
Cap	22	*16:28
Aqu	24	*23:15
Pis	27	*03:26
Ari	29	*06:07
Tau	31	*08:28
Gem	2	*11:23
Can	4	*15:22
Leo	6	*20:53
Vir	9	*04:24
Lib	11	*14:21
Sco	14	*02:24
Sag	16	*14:55
Cap	19	*01:29
Aqu	21	*08:31

1946		
Gem	24	*01:17
Can	26	*02:43
Leo	28	*03:57
Vir	30	*06:32
Lib	1	*12:05
Sco	3	*21:23
Sag	6	*09:36
Cap	8	*22:22
Aqu	11	*09:22
Pis	13	*17:40
Ari	15	*23:36
Tau	18	*03:58
Gem	20	*07:22
Can	22	*10:06

1947		
Lib	22	*14:34
Sco	24	*20:41
Sag	27	*06:40
Cap	29	*19:01
Aqu	1	*07:49
Pis	3	*19:48
Ari	6	*06:19
Tau	8	*14:42
Gem	10	*20:16
Can	12	*22:48
Leo	14	*23:05
Vir	16	*22:49
Lib	19	*00:05
Sco	21	*04:44

1948		
Pis	23	*18:12
Ari	26	*06:57
Tau	28	*18:33
Gem	31	*03:00
Can	2	*07:19
Leo	4	*08:12
Vir	6	*07:32
Lib	8	*07:30
Sco	10	*09:57
Sag	12	*15:49
Cap	15	*00:52
Aqu	17	*12:02
Pis	20	*00:23
Ari	22	*13:05

1949		
Can	23	*10:50
Leo	25	*15:18
Vir	27	*17:35
Lib	29	*19:19
Sco	31	*21:44
Sag	3	*01:25
Cap	5	*06:36
Aqu	7	*13:34
Pis	9	*22:46
Ari	12	*10:20
Tau	14	*23:17
Gem	17	*11:21
Can	19	*20:13
Leo	22	*01:06

♌ Leo – Finding Your Moon Sign ☽

1950		
Sco	22	*12:26
Sag	24	*14:54
Cap	26	*16:39
Aqu	28	*18:55
Pis	30	*23:19
Ari	2	*07:02
Tau	4	*18:05
Gem	7	*06:43
Can	9	*18:26
Leo	12	*03:35
Vir	14	*10:02
Lib	16	*14:30
Sco	18	*17:48
Sag	20	*20:35
Cap	22	*23:23

1951		
Ari	23	*07:21
Tau	25	*15:07
Gem	28	*02:07
Can	30	*14:42
Leo	2	*03:07
Vir	4	*14:17
Lib	6	*23:33
Sco	9	*06:23
Sag	11	*10:29
Cap	13	*12:17
Aqu	15	*12:53
Pis	17	*13:53
Ari	19	*16:58
Tau	21	*23:27

1952		
Leo	22	*01:20
Vir	24	*14:24
Lib	27	*02:53
Sco	29	*13:02
Sag	31	*19:36
Cap	2	*22:26
Aqu	4	*22:40
Pis	6	*22:05
Ari	8	*22:34
Tau	11	*01:46
Gem	13	*08:37
Can	15	*18:52
Leo	18	*07:18
Vir	20	*20:22

1953		
Cap	24	*04:05
Aqu	26	*07:02
Pis	28	*08:06
Ari	30	*08:55
Tau	1	*10:57
Gem	3	*15:11
Can	5	*22:00
Leo	8	*07:16
Vir	10	*18:33
Lib	13	*07:08
Sco	15	*19:43
Sag	18	*06:29
Cap	20	*13:51
Aqu	22	*17:28

1954		
Tau	23	*00:52
Gem	25	*03:30
Can	27	*06:41
Leo	29	*11:11
Vir	31	*17:49
Lib	3	*03:14
Sco	5	*15:02
Sag	8	*03:31
Cap	10	*14:19
Aqu	12	*21:53
Pis	15	*02:16
Ari	17	*04:37
Tau	19	*06:25
Gem	21	*08:56

♌ Leo – Finding Your Moon Sign ☽

1955		
Lib	24	*01:17
Sco	26	*10:19
Sag	28	*22:24
Cap	31	*11:18
Aqu	2	*22:50
Pis	5	*08:03
Ari	7	*14:59
Tau	9	*20:02
Gem	11	*23:32
Can	14	*01:50
Leo	16	*03:34
Vir	18	*05:57
Lib	20	*10:34
Sco	22	*18:37

1956		
Aqu	22	*21:28
Pis	25	*09:49
Ari	27	*20:53
Tau	30	*05:39
Gem	1	*11:14
Can	3	*13:31
Leo	5	*13:26
Vir	7	*12:50
Lib	9	*13:51
Sco	11	*18:20
Sag	14	*03:00
Cap	16	*14:47
Aqu	19	*03:37
Pis	21	*15:46

1957		
Gem	22	*16:33
Can	24	*21:03
Leo	26	*22:15
Vir	28	*21:59
Lib	30	*22:20
Sco	2	*01:01
Sag	4	*06:47
Cap	6	*15:23
Aqu	9	*02:01
Pis	11	*14:02
Ari	14	*02:45
Tau	16	*14:59
Gem	19	*00:49
Can	21	*06:48

1958		
Sco	23	*13:57
Sag	25	*17:25
Cap	27	*21:53
Aqu	30	*03:52
Pis	1	*12:12
Ari	3	*23:14
Tau	6	*12:03
Gem	9	*00:15
Can	11	*09:23
Leo	13	*14:42
Vir	15	*17:06
Lib	17	*18:16
Sco	19	*19:49
Sag	21	*22:48

1959		
Pis	22	*12:42
Ari	24	*19:53
Tau	27	*06:43
Gem	29	*19:23
Can	1	*07:23
Leo	3	*17:08
Vir	6	*00:28
Lib	8	*05:56
Sco	10	*09:59
Sag	12	*12:57
Cap	14	*15:18
Aqu	16	*17:53
Pis	18	*22:00
Ari	21	*04:51

♌ Leo – Finding Your Moon Sign ☽

1960
Leo	23	*16:45
Vir	26	*04:31
Lib	28	*14:32
Sco	30	*21:53
Sag	2	*02:02
Cap	4	*03:25
Aqu	6	*03:20
Pis	8	*03:42
Ari	10	*06:21
Tau	12	*12:36
Gem	14	*22:29
Can	17	*10:42
Leo	19	*23:17
Vir	22	*10:40

1961
Sag	23	*09:40
Cap	25	*12:27
Aqu	27	*12:40
Pis	29	*12:13
Ari	31	*12:56
Tau	2	*16:19
Gem	4	*23:04
Can	7	*08:56
Leo	9	*20:59
Vir	12	*10:00
Lib	14	*22:43
Sco	17	*09:43
Sag	19	*17:43
Cap	21	*22:05

1962
Ari	22	*00:33
Tau	24	*02:57
Gem	26	*06:56
Can	28	*13:00
Leo	30	*21:21
Vir	2	*07:57
Lib	4	*20:17
Sco	7	*08:55
Sag	9	*19:47
Cap	12	*03:16
Aqu	14	*07:06
Pis	16	*08:16
Ari	18	*08:25
Tau	20	*09:20
Gem	22	*12:28

1963
Vir	23	*07:06
Lib	25	*16:02
Sco	28	*03:38
Sag	30	*16:07
Cap	2	*03:11
Aqu	4	*11:24
Pis	6	*16:45
Ari	8	*20:06
Tau	10	*22:37
Gem	13	*01:15
Can	15	*04:39
Leo	17	*09:17
Vir	19	*15:40
Lib	22	*00:26

1964
Cap	22	*00:26
Aqu	24	*12:29
Pis	26	*22:34
Ari	29	*06:25
Tau	31	*11:59
Gem	2	*15:27
Can	4	*17:12
Leo	6	*18:10
Vir	8	*19:50
Lib	10	*23:52
Sco	13	*07:31
Sag	15	*18:44
Cap	18	*07:37
Aqu	20	*19:38

♌ Leo – Finding Your Moon Sign ☽

1965			1966			1967			1968			1969		
Gem	24	*01:46	Lib	22	*13:38	Pis	24	*01:28	Can	22	*20:30	Sco	22	*13:02
Can	26	*03:52	Sco	24	*16:32	Ari	26	*12:00	Leo	25	*06:54	Sag	24	*17:10
Leo	28	*03:36	Sag	26	*22:05	Tau	29	*00:40	Vir	27	*15:09	Cap	26	*18:09
Vir	30	*02:55	Cap	29	*06:04	Gem	31	*12:59	Lib	29	*21:31	Aqu	28	*17:34
Lib	1	*03:54	Aqu	31	*16:01	Can	2	*22:30	Sco	1	*02:10	Pis	30	*17:30
Sco	3	*08:21	Pis	3	*03:35	Leo	5	*04:25	Sag	3	*05:10	Ari	1	*19:55
Sag	5	*16:49	Ari	5	*16:14	Vir	7	*07:35	Cap	5	*06:57	Tau	4	*02:02
Cap	8	*04:22	Tau	8	*04:37	Lib	9	*09:34	Aqu	7	*08:37	Gem	6	*11:50
Aqu	10	*17:09	Gem	10	*14:37	Sco	11	*11:44	Pis	9	*11:46	Can	8	*23:57
Pis	13	*05:37	Can	12	*20:40	Sag	13	*14:52	Ari	11	*17:52	Leo	11	*12:37
Ari	15	*16:56	Leo	14	*22:48	Cap	15	*19:18	Tau	14	*03:36	Vir	14	*00:31
Tau	18	*02:26	Vir	16	*22:34	Aqu	18	*01:17	Gem	16	*15:51	Lib	16	*10:50
Gem	20	*09:19	Lib	18	*22:05	Pis	20	*09:18	Can	19	*04:14	Sco	18	*18:53
Can	22	*13:03	Sco	20	*23:25	Ari	22	*19:47	Leo	21	*14:38	Sag	21	*00:10

♌ Leo – Finding Your Moon Sign ☽

1970		
Ari	23	*03:43
Tau	25	*07:18
Gem	27	*13:53
Can	29	*23:14
Leo	1	*10:44
Vir	3	*23:34
Lib	6	*12:32
Sco	8	*23:55
Sag	11	*08:06
Cap	13	*12:23
Aqu	15	*13:30
Pis	17	*13:01
Ari	19	*12:50
Tau	21	*14:46

1971		
Leo	22	*11:17
Vir	24	*21:09
Lib	27	*09:11
Sco	29	*21:49
Sag	1	*08:48
Cap	3	*16:31
Aqu	5	*20:45
Pis	7	*22:33
Ari	9	*23:26
Tau	12	*00:56
Gem	14	*04:10
Can	16	*09:50
Leo	18	*17:57
Vir	21	*04:18

1972		
Cap	23	*16:09
Aqu	26	*01:06
Pis	28	*07:28
Ari	30	*11:49
Tau	1	*14:57
Gem	3	*17:33
Can	5	*20:17
Leo	7	*23:56
Vir	10	*05:22
Lib	12	*13:28
Sco	15	*00:19
Sag	17	*12:48
Cap	20	*00:36
Aqu	22	*09:41

1973		
Tau	23	*03:40
Gem	25	*06:57
Can	27	*08:09
Leo	29	*08:29
Vir	31	*09:35
Lib	2	*13:13
Sco	4	*20:36
Sag	7	*07:36
Cap	9	*20:29
Aqu	12	*08:51
Pis	14	*19:13
Ari	17	*03:15
Tau	19	*09:13
Gem	21	*13:25

1974		
Lib	23	*18:18
Sco	25	*22:46
Sag	28	*06:59
Cap	30	*18:10
Aqu	2	*06:46
Pis	4	*19:26
Ari	7	*07:14
Tau	9	*17:12
Gem	12	*00:13
Can	14	*03:47
Leo	16	*04:26
Vir	18	*03:42
Lib	20	*03:45
Sco	22	*06:37

♌ Leo – Finding Your Moon Sign ☽

1975		
Aqu	23	*05:55
Pis	25	*16:58
Ari	28	*05:27
Tau	30	*17:53
Gem	2	*04:01
Can	4	*10:15
Leo	6	*12:42
Vir	8	*12:53
Lib	10	*12:51
Sco	12	*14:30
Sag	14	*18:59
Cap	17	*02:25
Aqu	19	*12:09
Pis	21	*23:32

1976		
Gem	22	*01:39
Can	24	*11:38
Leo	26	*18:18
Vir	28	*22:22
Lib	31	*01:13
Sco	2	*03:55
Sag	4	*07:03
Cap	6	*10:54
Aqu	8	*15:57
Pis	10	*23:01
Ari	13	*08:49
Tau	15	*21:05
Gem	18	*09:53
Can	20	*20:32

1977		
Sco	23	*18:13
Sag	25	*21:03
Cap	27	*22:14
Aqu	29	*23:04
Pis	1	*01:24
Ari	3	*06:54
Tau	5	*16:18
Gem	8	*04:29
Can	10	*17:03
Leo	13	*03:56
Vir	15	*12:24
Lib	17	*18:48
Sco	19	*23:34
Sag	22	*03:02

1978		
Pis	22	*07:26
Ari	24	*09:46
Tau	26	*15:51
Gem	29	*01:31
Can	31	*13:28
Leo	3	*02:10
Vir	5	*14:28
Lib	8	*01:28
Sco	10	*10:10
Sag	12	*15:41
Cap	14	*18:02
Aqu	16	*18:14
Pis	18	*18:04
Ari	20	*19:29

1979		
Leo	24	*00:30
Vir	26	*13:01
Lib	29	*02:05
Sco	31	*13:45
Sag	2	*22:04
Cap	5	*02:21
Aqu	7	*03:27
Pis	9	*03:05
Ari	11	*03:10
Tau	13	*05:21
Gem	15	*10:42
Can	17	*19:17
Leo	20	*06:28
Vir	22	*19:11

♌ Leo – Finding Your Moon Sign ☽

1980		
Sag	22	*21:41
Cap	25	*05:44
Aqu	27	*10:33
Pis	29	*13:10
Ari	31	*14:53
Tau	2	*16:54
Gem	4	*20:10
Can	7	*01:12
Leo	9	*08:23
Vir	11	*17:54
Lib	14	*05:32
Sco	16	*18:14
Sag	19	*06:07
Cap	21	*15:10

1981		
Ari	22	*03:43
Tau	24	*07:18
Gem	26	*09:41
Can	28	*11:41
Leo	30	*14:20
Vir	1	*18:54
Lib	4	*02:24
Sco	6	*12:58
Sag	9	*01:22
Cap	11	*13:19
Aqu	13	*22:55
Pis	16	*05:34
Ari	18	*09:48
Tau	20	*12:43
Gem	22	*15:18

1982		
Vir	22	*23:21
Lib	25	*02:46
Sco	27	*09:59
Sag	29	*20:48
Cap	1	*09:35
Aqu	3	*22:16
Pis	6	*09:22
Ari	8	*18:20
Tau	11	*00:59
Gem	13	*05:21
Can	15	*07:40
Leo	17	*08:39
Vir	19	*09:40
Lib	21	*12:23

1983		
Cap	22	*08:11
Aqu	24	*20:26
Pis	27	*09:11
Ari	29	*21:20
Tau	1	*07:36
Gem	3	*14:41
Can	5	*18:08
Leo	7	*18:36
Vir	9	*17:48
Lib	11	*17:51
Sco	13	*20:44
Sag	16	*03:34
Cap	18	*13:59
Aqu	21	*02:25

1984		
Gem	23	*17:09
Can	25	*23:42
Leo	28	*02:40
Vir	30	*03:28
Lib	1	*04:03
Sco	3	*06:03
Sag	5	*10:30
Cap	7	*17:24
Aqu	10	*02:25
Pis	12	*13:13
Ari	15	*01:28
Tau	17	*14:12
Gem	20	*01:30
Can	22	*09:18

♌ Leo – Finding Your Moon Sign ☽

1985			1986			1987			1988			1989		
Lib	22	*17:09	Pis	23	*14:59	Can	23	*03:13	Sco	22	*03:12	Ari	23	*06:40
Sco	24	*20:15	Ari	25	*20:03	Leo	25	*15:49	Sag	24	*11:40	Tau	25	*09:10
Sag	26	*23:12	Tau	28	*05:11	Vir	28	*04:25	Cap	26	*16:06	Gem	27	*12:15
Cap	29	*02:21	Gem	30	*17:19	Lib	30	*15:59	Aqu	28	*17:24	Can	29	*16:31
Aqu	31	*06:25	Can	2	*06:03	Sco	2	*01:08	Pis	30	*17:22	Leo	31	*22:41
Pis	2	*12:34	Leo	4	*17:26	Sag	4	*06:46	Ari	1	*17:53	Vir	3	*07:19
Ari	4	*21:43	Vir	7	*02:43	Cap	6	*08:50	Tau	3	*20:24	Lib	5	*18:28
Tau	7	*09:41	Lib	9	*10:03	Aqu	8	*08:36	Gem	6	*01:43	Sco	8	*07:04
Gem	9	*22:30	Sco	11	*15:35	Pis	10	*08:01	Can	8	*09:52	Sag	10	*19:01
Can	12	*09:27	Sag	13	*19:16	Ari	12	*09:10	Leo	10	*20:26	Cap	13	*04:15
Leo	14	*16:56	Cap	15	*21:22	Tau	14	*13:39	Vir	13	*08:45	Aqu	15	*09:57
Vir	16	*21:14	Aqu	17	*22:44	Gem	16	*21:59	Lib	15	*21:51	Pis	17	*12:44
Lib	18	*23:43	Pis	20	*00:52	Can	19	*09:19	Sco	18	*10:10	Ari	19	*13:58
Sco	21	*01:51	Ari	22	*05:27	Leo	21	*21:57	Sag	20	*19:53	Tau	21	*15:10

♌ Leo – Finding Your Moon Sign ☽

1990		
Leo	22	*04:28
Vir	24	*08:18
Lib	26	*15:19
Sco	29	*01:39
Sag	31	*13:59
Cap	3	*02:07
Aqu	5	*12:18
Pis	7	*19:53
Ari	10	*01:12
Tau	12	*04:54
Gem	14	*07:41
Can	16	*10:12
Leo	18	*13:11
Vir	20	*17:33

1991		
Cap	23	*22:55
Aqu	26	*11:48
Pis	28	*23:33
Ari	31	*09:19
Tau	2	*16:31
Gem	4	*20:53
Can	6	*22:46
Leo	8	*23:09
Vir	10	*23:35
Lib	13	*01:53
Sco	15	*07:34
Sag	17	*17:10
Cap	20	*05:34
Aqu	22	*18:26

1992		
Tau	22	*21:34
Gem	25	*04:43
Can	27	*08:07
Leo	29	*08:38
Vir	31	*08:01
Lib	2	*08:17
Sco	4	*11:17
Sag	6	*17:56
Cap	9	*04:00
Aqu	11	*16:06
Pis	14	*04:50
Ari	16	*17:11
Tau	19	*04:09
Gem	21	*12:34

1993		
Lib	23	*19:39
Sco	25	*22:00
Sag	28	*02:13
Cap	30	*08:26
Aqu	1	*16:36
Pis	4	*02:43
Ari	6	*14:39
Tau	9	*03:22
Gem	11	*14:45
Can	13	*22:44
Leo	16	*02:42
Vir	18	*03:40
Lib	20	*03:35
Sco	22	*04:27

1994		
Aqu	22	*20:38
Pis	25	*01:57
Ari	27	*10:31
Tau	29	*22:13
Gem	1	*11:04
Can	3	*22:21
Leo	6	*06:30
Vir	8	*11:41
Lib	10	*15:06
Sco	12	*17:55
Sag	14	*20:53
Cap	17	*00:18
Aqu	19	*04:33
Pis	21	*10:28

♌ Leo – Finding Your Moon Sign ☽

1995		
Gem	22	*06:23
Can	24	*19:15
Leo	27	*07:06
Vir	29	*17:11
Lib	1	*01:22
Sco	3	*07:28
Sag	5	*11:13
Cap	7	*12:51
Aqu	9	*13:27
Pis	11	*14:46
Ari	13	*18:40
Tau	16	*02:26
Gem	18	*13:40
Can	21	*02:23

1996		
Sco	23	*15:41
Sag	25	*21:22
Cap	27	*23:16
Aqu	29	*22:47
Pis	31	*22:01
Ari	2	*23:06
Tau	5	*03:34
Gem	7	*11:49
Can	9	*22:57
Leo	12	*11:28
Vir	15	*00:06
Lib	17	*11:54
Sco	19	*21:49
Sag	22	*04:47

1997		
Pis	22	*07:59
Ari	24	*09:03
Tau	26	*11:54
Gem	28	*17:04
Can	31	*00:38
Leo	2	*10:27
Vir	4	*22:15
Lib	7	*11:16
Sco	9	*23:49
Sag	12	*09:43
Cap	14	*15:41
Aqu	16	*17:58
Pis	18	*18:00
Ari	20	*17:44
Tau	22	*18:57

1998		
Leo	23	*12:49
Vir	25	*20:34
Lib	28	*07:14
Sco	30	*19:44
Sag	2	*07:47
Cap	4	*17:17
Aqu	6	*23:29
Pis	9	*03:03
Ari	11	*05:10
Tau	13	*07:04
Gem	15	*09:46
Can	17	*13:55
Leo	19	*20:00
Vir	22	*04:21

1999		
Sag	23	*02:48
Cap	25	*15:07
Aqu	28	*01:53
Pis	30	*10:26
Ari	1	*16:46
Tau	3	*21:08
Gem	5	*23:56
Can	8	*01:52
Leo	10	*03:55
Vir	12	*07:21
Lib	14	*13:24
Sco	16	*22:40
Sag	19	*10:31
Cap	21	*22:58

2000		
Ari	22	*00:08
Tau	24	*07:42
Gem	26	*12:00
Can	28	*13:28
Leo	30	*13:23
Vir	1	*13:27
Lib	3	*15:32
Sco	5	*21:05
Sag	8	*06:30
Cap	10	*18:43
Aqu	13	*07:42
Pis	15	*19:40
Ari	18	*05:43
Tau	20	*13:29
Gem	22	*18:54

♌ Leo Mercury Signs ☿

DATES	CANCER	LEO	VIRGO
1930		22 Jul–4 Aug	4 Aug–23 Aug
1931		22 Jul–28 Jul	28 Jul–23 Aug
1932		22 Jul–27 Jul	27 Jul–10 Aug
		10 Aug–23 Aug	
1933	22 Jul–23 Aug		
1934	22 Jul–9 Aug	9 Aug–23 Aug	
1935	22 Jul–2 Aug	2 Aug–16 Aug	16 Aug–23 Aug
1936	23 Jul	23 Jul–7 Aug	7 Aug–23 Aug
1937		22 Jul–31 Jul	31 Jul–23 Aug
1938		22 Jul–26 Jul	26 Jul–23 Aug
1939		22 Jul–23 Aug	
1940		22 Jul–11 Aug	11 Aug–23 Aug
1941	22 Jul–6 Aug	6 Aug–21 Aug	21 Aug–23 Aug
1942	23 Jul–29 Jul	29 Jul–13 Aug	13 Aug–23 Aug
1943		22 Jul–5 Aug	5 Aug–23 Aug
1944		22 Jul–28 Jul	28 Jul–23 Aug
1945		22 Jul–26 Jul	26 Jul–17 Aug
		17 Aug–23 Aug	
1946		22 Jul–23 Aug	
1947	22 Jul–10 Aug	10 Aug–23 Aug	
1948	22 Jul–2 Aug	2 Aug–17 Aug	17 Aug–23 Aug
1949	22 Jul– 25 Jul	25 Jul– 23 Aug	
1950		22 Jul–2 Aug	2 Aug–23 Aug
1951		22 Jul–27 Jul	27 Jul–23 Aug
1952		22 Jul–23 Aug	
1953	28 Jul–11 Aug	22 Jul–28 Jul	11 Aug–23 Aug
1954	22 Jul–7 Aug	7 Aug–23 Aug	23 Aug
1955	23 Jul–30 Jul	30 Jul–14 Aug	14 Aug–23 Aug
1956		22 Jul–5 Aug	5 Aug–23 Aug

DATES	CANCER	LEO	VIRGO
1957		22 Jul–26 Jul	26 Jul–23 Aug
1958		22 Jul–26 Jul	26 Jul–23 Aug
1959		22 Jul–23 Aug	
1960	22 Jul–10 Aug	10 Aug–23 Aug	
1961	22 Jul–4 Aug	4Aug–18 Aug	18 Aug–23 Aug
1962	22 Jul–26 Jul	26 Jul–10 Aug	10 Aug–23 Aug
1963		22 Jul–3 Aug	3 Aug–23 Aug
1964		22 Jul–27 Jul	27 Jul–23 Aug
1965	22 Jul–31 Jul	31 Jul -3 Aug	3 Aug–23 Aug
1966		22 Jul–23 Aug	
1967	22 Jul–8 Aug	8 Aug–23 Aug	
1968	22 Jul–31 Jul	31 Jul–15 Aug	15 Aug–23 Aug
1969		22 Jul–7 Jul	7 Jul–23 Aug
1970		22 Jul–26 Jul	26 Jul–23 Aug
1971		22 Jul–26 Jul	26 Jul–23 Aug
1972		22 Jul–23 Aug	
1973	22 Jul–11 Aug	11 Aug–23 Aug	
1974	22 Jul–5 Aug	5 Aug–20 Aug	20 Aug–23 Aug
1975		22 Jul–3 Aug	3 Aug–23 Aug
1976		22 Jul–3 Aug	3 Aug–23 Aug
1977		22 Jul–28 Jul	28 Jul–23 Aug
1978		22 Jul–27 Jul	27 Jul–23 Aug
1979		22 Jul–23 Aug	
1980	22 Jul–9 Aug	9 Aug–23 Aug	
1981	22 Jul–1 Aug	1 Aug–16 Aug	16 Aug–23 Aug
1982	22 Jul–24 Jul	24 Jul–8 Aug	8 Aug–23 Aug
1983		22 Jul–1 Aug	1 Aug–23 Aug
1984		22 Jul–26 Jul	26 Jul–23 Aug
1985		22 Jul–23 Aug	
1986	23 Jul–11 Aug	23 Jul	
		11 Aug–23 Aug	
1987	23 Jul–6 Aug	6 Aug–21 Aug	21 Aug–23 Aug

DATES	CANCER	LEO	VIRGO
1988	22 Jul–28 Jul	28 Jul–12 Aug	12 Aug–23 Aug
1989		22 Jul–5 Aug	5 Aug–23 Aug
1990		22 Jul–29 Jul	29 Jul–23 Aug
1991		22 Jul–26 Jul	26 Jul–19 Aug
		19 Aug–23 Aug	
1992		22 Jul–23 Aug	
1993	22 Jul–10 Aug	10 Aug–23 Aug	
1994	22 Jul–3 Aug	3 Aug–18 Aug	18 Aug–23 Aug
1995	22 Jul–25 Jul	25 Jul–10 Aug	10 Aug–23 Aug
1996		22 Jul–1 Aug	1 Aug–23 Aug
1997		22 Jul–27 Jul	27 Jul–23 Aug ·
1998		22 Jul–23 Aug	
1999	22 Jul–31 Jul	31 Jul–11 Aug	
		11 Aug–23 Aug	
2000	22 Jul–7 Aug	7 Aug–23 Aug	23 Aug

♌ Leo Venus Signs ♀

YEAR	GEMINI	CANCER	LEO	VIRGO	LIBRA
1930		22 Jul–3 Aug	3 Aug–23 Aug	22 Jul–10 Aug	10 Aug–23 Aug
1931		28 Jul–23 Aug			
1932	22 Jul–28 Jul		22 Jul–27 Jul	27 Jul–21 Aug	21 Aug–23 Aug
1933		22 Jul–17 Aug	17 Aug–23 Aug		
1934	22 Jul				
1935				22 Jul–23 Aug	
1936			22 Jul–11 Aug	11 Aug–23 Aug	
1937	22 Jul–4 Aug	4 Aug–23 Aug			
1938				22 Jul–9 Aug	9 Aug–23 Aug
1939		22 Jul–2 Aug	2 Aug–23 Aug		
1940	22 Jul–1 Aug	1 Aug–23 Aug			
1941			22 Jul–27 Jul	27 Jul–21 Aug	21 Aug–23 Aug
1942		22 Jul–17 Aug	17 Aug–23 Aug		
1943				22 Jul–23 Aug	
1944			22 Jul–10 Aug	10 Aug–23 Aug	
1945	22 Jul–4 Aug	4 Aug–23 Aug			
1946				22 Jul–9 Aug	9 Aug–23 Aug
1947		22 Jul–2 Aug	2 Aug–23 Aug		
1948	22 Jul–3 Aug	3 Aug–23 Aug			
1949			22 Jul–26 Jul	26 Jul–20 Aug	
1950			16 Aug–23 Aug		20 Aug–23 Aug
1951		22 Jul–16 Aug		22 Jul–23 Aug	

YEAR	GEMINI	CANCER	LEO	VIRGO	LIBRA
1952	22 Jul–4 Aug		22 Jul–9 Aug	9 Aug–23 Aug	
1953		4 Aug–23 Aug		22 Jul–9 Aug	9 Aug–23 Aug
1954			1 Aug–23 Aug		
1955		22 Jul–1 Aug			
1956	22 Jul–4 Aug	4 Aug–23 Aug			
1957			22 Jul–26 Jul	26 Jul–20 Aug	20 Aug–23 Aug
1958		22 Jul–16 Aug	16 Aug–23 Aug		
1959				22 Jul–23 Aug	
1960			22 Jul–9 Aug	9 Aug–23 Aug	
1961	22 Jul–3 Aug	3 Aug–23 Aug			
1962				22 Jul–8 Aug	8 Aug–23 Aug
1963		22 Jul–31 Jul	31 Jul–23 Aug		
1964	22 Jul–5 Aug	5 Aug–23 Aug			
1965			22 Jul–25 Jul	25 Jul–19 Aug	19 Aug–23 Aug
1966		22 Jul–15 Aug	15 Aug–23 Aug	22 Jul–23 Aug	
1967				8 Aug–23 Aug	
1968			22 Jul–8 Aug		
1969	22 Jul–3 Aug	3 Aug–23 Aug		22 Jul–8 Aug	8 Aug–23 Aug
1970			31 Jul–23 Aug		
1971		22 Jul–31 Jul			
1972	22 Jul–6 Aug	6 Aug–23 Aug	22 Jul–25 Jul		
1973			14 Aug–23 Aug	25 Jul–19 Aug	19 Aug–23 Aug
1974		22 Jul–14 Aug			
1975				22 Jul–23 Aug	
1976			22 Jul–8 Aug	8 Aug–23 Aug	

117

YEAR	GEMINI	CANCER	LEO	VIRGO	LIBRA
1977	22 Jul–2 Aug	2 Aug–23 Aug			
1978				22 Jul–8 Aug	8 Aug–23 Aug
1979		22 Jul–30 Jul	30 Jul–23 Aug		
1980	22 Jul–6 Aug	6 Aug–23 Aug			18 Aug–23 Aug
1981		22 Jul–14 Aug	22 Jul–24 Jul	24 Jul–18 Aug	
1982			14 Aug–23 Aug		
1983				22 Jul–23 Aug	
1984				7 Aug–23 Aug	
1985	22 Jul–2 Aug	2 Aug–23 Aug	22 Jul–7 Aug		7 Aug–23 Aug
1986				22 Jul–7 Aug	
1987		22 Jul–30 Jul	30 Jul–23 Aug	23 Aug	
1988	22 Jul–24 Jul	24 Jul–18 Aug	18 Aug–23 Aug		18 Aug–23 Aug
1989			22 Jul–24 Jul	24 Jul–18 Aug	
1990		22 Jul–13 Aug	13 Aug–23 Aug		21 Aug–23 Aug
1991				22 Jul–21 Aug	
1992				7 Aug–23 Aug	
1993	22 Jul–1 Aug	1 Aug–23 Aug	22 Jul–7 Aug		7 Aug–23 Aug
1994				22 Jul–7 Aug	
1995		22 Jul–29 Jul	29 Jul–23 Aug	23 Aug	
1996	22 Jul–7 Aug	7 Aug–23 Aug			
1997				22 Jul–17 Aug	17 Aug–23 Aug
1998		22 Jul–13 Aug	13 Aug–23 Aug		15 Aug–23 Aug
1999				22 Jul–15 Aug	
2000			22 Jul–6 Aug	6 Aug–23 Aug	

The Leo Workbook

There are no right or wrong answers in this chapter. Its aim is to help you assess how you are doing with your life – in YOUR estimation – and to make the material of this book more personal and, I hope, more helpful for you.

1. The Leo in You
Which of the following Leo characteristics do you recognise in yourself?

confident	dignified	dramatic
entertaining	fun-loving	generous
loyal	majestic	radiant
spontaneous	sunny-natured	warm-hearted

2. In which situations do you find yourself acting like this?

_____

_____

3. When you are feeling vulnerable, you may show some of the less constructive Leo traits. Do you recognise yourself in any of the following?

condescending	domineering	extravagant
presumptious	lazy	pompous
arrogant	self-absorbed	vain

What kind of situations trigger off this behaviour and what do you think might help you, in these situations, to respond more positively?

_____

_____

4. You and Your Roles

a) Where, if anywhere, in your life do you play the role of Performer?

_____

_____

b) What role or roles do you perform?

_____

_____

5. Do you play any of the following roles – in the literal or broad sense – in any part of your life? If not, would you like to? What might be your first step towards doing so?

Ruler	Organiser	Star
Director	Ambassador	Dramatist

_____

_____

6. Sun Aspects

If any of the following planets aspects your Sun, add each of the keywords for that planet to complete the following sentences. Which phrases ring true for you?

I am _____

My father is _____

My job requires that I am _____

Saturn Words (Use only if your Sun is aspected by Saturn)

ambitious	controlling	judgmental	mature
serious	strict	traditional	bureaucratic
cautious	committed	hard-working	disciplined
depressive	responsible	status-seeking	limiting

Uranus Words (Use only if your Sun is aspected by Uranus)

freedom-loving	progressive	rebellious	shocking
scientific	cutting-edge	detached	contrary
friendly	disruptive	eccentric	humanitarian
innovative	nonconformist	unconventional	exciting

Neptune Words (Use only if your Sun is aspected by Neptune)

sensitive	idealistic	artistic	impressionable
disappointing	impractical	escapist	self-sacrificing
spiritual	unrealistic	dreamy	glamorous
dependent	deceptive	rescuing	blissful

Pluto Words (Use only if your Sun is aspected by Pluto)

powerful	single-minded	intense	extreme
secretive	rotten	passionate	mysterious
investigative	uncompromising	ruthless	wealthy
abusive	regenerative	associated with sex, birth or death	

a) If one or more negative words describe you or your job, how might you turn that quality into something more positive or satisfying?

_____
_____

7. The Moon and You

Below are brief lists of what the Moon needs, in the various elements, to feel secure and satisfied. First find your Moon element, then estimate how much of each of the following you are expressing and receiving in your life, especially at home and in your relationships, on a scale of 0 to 5 where 0 = none and 5 = plenty.

FIRE MOONS — Aries, Leo, Sagittarius

attention	action	drama
recognition	self-expression	spontaneity
enthusiasm	adventure	leadership

EARTH MOONS — Taurus, Virgo, Capricorn

stability	orderly routine	sensual pleasures
material security	a sense of rootedness	control over your home life
regular body care	practical achievements	pleasurable practical tasks

AIR MOONS — Gemini, Libra, Aquarius

mental rapport	stimulating ideas	emotional space
friendship	social justice	interesting conversations
fairness	socialising	freedom to circulate

WATER MOONS — Cancer, Scorpio, Pisces

intimacy	a sense of belonging	emotional rapport
emotional safety	respect for your feelings	time and space to retreat
acceptance	cherishing and being cherished	warmth and comfort

a) Do you feel your Moon is being 'fed' enough?

yes_____ no_____

b) How might you satisfy your Moon needs even better?

_____

_____

8. You and Your Mercury
As a Leo, your Mercury can only be in Cancer, Leo or Virgo. Below are some of the ways and situations in which Mercury in each of the elements might learn and communicate effectively. First find your Mercury sign, then circle the words you think apply to you.

Mercury in Fire (Leo)
action	imagination	identifying with the subject matter
excitement	drama	playing with possibilities

Mercury in Earth (Virgo)
time-tested methods	useful facts	well-structured information
'how to' instructions	demonstrations	hands-on experience

Mercury in Air (As a Leo, you can never have Mercury in an air sign; the words are included here for completeness)
facts arranged in categories	logic	demonstrable connections
rational arguments	theories	debate and sharing of ideas

Mercury in Water (Cancer)
pictures and images	charged atmospheres	feeling-linked information
intuitive understanding	emotional rapport	being shown personally

a) This game with Mercury can be done with a friend or on your own. Skim through a magazine until you find a picture that interests you. Then describe the picture – to your friend, or in writing or on tape. Notice what you emphasise and the kind of words you use. Now try to describe it using the language and emphasis of each of the other Mercury modes. How easy did you find that? Identifying the preferred Mercury style of others and using that style yourself can lead to improved communication all round.

9. Your Venus Values

Below are lists of qualities and situations that your Venus sign might enjoy. Assess on a scale of 0 to 5 how much your Venus desires and pleasures are met and expressed in your life. 0 = not at all, 5 = fully.

Venus in Gemini

You will activate your Venus through anything that stimulates your mind and uses a talent for making connections, for example:

playing go-between	flirting	talking and writing
passing on new ideas	witty use of words	trend-spotting

Venus in Cancer

You will activate your Venus through anything that makes you feel wise, intuitive, nurturing and nurtured, and at the centre of a 'family', for example:

a beautiful home	tenderness	sharing meals with loved ones
sharing feelings safely	home comforts	your family or country history

Venus in Leo

You will activate your Venus through anything that makes you feel special, unique, radiant and generous, for example:

extravagant gestures	luxury goods	prestigious activities
being central in a drama	acting nobly	being in love

Venus in Virgo

You will activate your Venus through anything that engages your powers of discrimination, for example:

restoring order	improving efficiency	using your skills
purifying your mind, body or environment	being of service	quality work

Venus in Libra

You will activate your Venus through anything cultured, balanced and fair, for example:

harmonious relationships	elegant surroundings	dressing well
courteous manners	artistic pursuits	political justice

a) How, and where, might you have more fun and pleasure by bringing more of what your Venus sign loves into your life?

_____

_____

b) Make a note here of the kind of gifts your Venus sign would love to receive. Then go on and spoil yourself . . .

_____

_____

Resources

Finding an Astrologer

I'm often asked what is the best way to find a reputable astrologer. Personal recommendation by someone whose judgement you trust is by far the best way. Ideally, the astrologer should also be endorsed by a reputable organisation whose members adhere to a strict code of ethics, which guarantees confidentiality and professional conduct.

Contact Addresses

Association of Professional Astrologers International
www.professionalastrologers.org

APAI members adhere to a strict code of professional ethics.

Astrological Association of Great Britain
www.astrologicalassociation.co.uk

The main body for astrology in the UK, with links to similar organisations throughout the world.

Faculty of Astrological Studies
www.astrology.org.uk

The teaching body internationally recognised for excellence in astrological education at all levels.

Jane Ridder-Patrick
www.janeridderpatrick.com

Your Leo Friends

You can keep a record of Cancerians you know here, with the page numbers of where to find their descriptions handy for future reference.

Name _____ Date of Birth _____

Aspects*	None	Saturn	Uranus	Neptune	Pluto

Moon Sign _____ p _____
Mercury Sign _____ p _____
Venus Sign _____ p _____

Name _____ Date of Birth _____

Aspects*	None	Saturn	Uranus	Neptune	Pluto

Moon Sign _____ p _____
Mercury Sign _____ p _____
Venus Sign _____ p _____

Name _____ Date of Birth _____

Aspects*	None	Saturn	Uranus	Neptune	Pluto

Moon Sign _____ p _____
Mercury Sign _____ p _____
Venus Sign _____ p _____

Name _____ Date of Birth _____

Aspects*	None	Saturn	Uranus	Neptune	Pluto

Moon Sign _____ p _____
Mercury Sign _____ p _____
Venus Sign _____ p _____

* Circle where applicable

Sign Summaries

SIGN	GLYPH	APPROX DATES	SYMBOL	ROLE	ELEMENT	QUALITY	PLANET	GLYPH	KEYWORD
1. Aries	♈	21/3 – 19/4	Ram	Hero	Fire	Cardinal	Mars	♂	Assertiveness
2. Taurus	♉	20/4 – 20/5	Bull	Steward	Earth	Fixed	Venus	♀	Stability
3. Gemini	♊	21/5 – 21/6	Twins	Go-Between	Air	Mutable	Mercury	☿	Communication
4. Cancer	♋	22/6 – 22/7	Crab	Caretaker	Water	Cardinal	Moon	☽	Nurture
5. Leo	♌	23/7 – 22/8	Lion	Performer	Fire	Fixed	Sun	☉	Glory
6. Virgo	♍	23/8 – 22/9	Maiden	Craftworker	Earth	Mutable	Mercury	☿	Skill
7. Libra	♎	23/9 – 22/10	Scales	Architect	Air	Cardinal	Venus	♀	Balance
8. Scorpio	♏	23/10 – 23/11	Scorpion	Survivor	Water	Fixed	Pluto	♇	Transformation
9. Sagittarius	♐	22/11 – 21/12	Archer	Adventurer	Fire	Mutable	Jupiter	♃	Wisdom
10. Capricorn	♑	22/12 – 19/1	Goat	Manager	Earth	Cardinal	Saturn	♄	Responsibility
11. Aquarius	♒	20/1 – 19/2	Waterbearer	Scientist	Air	Fixed	Uranus	♅	Progress
12. Pisces	♓	20/2 – 20/3	Fishes	Dreamer	Water	Mutable	Neptune	♆	Universality